MW01256541

2005

A DAREDEVIL
&
TWO BOARDS

BY GREGOR ZIEMER

Copyright 2005

Hunter Halverson Press, LLC

Cover and layout design by Ann Christianson, Radius Creative.

Edited by Rebecca Wasieleski

Photos courtesy of Bob Parrott, *Lake City Graphic*, unless otherwise indicated.

Printed by McNaughton & Gunn, Saline, Michigan.

United States of America

First Edition

ISBN-13: 978-0-9744143-1-7

ISBN-10: 0-9744143-1-X

All rights reserved. No part of this publication may be reproduced or transmitted in any form or by any means, electronic or mechanical, including photocopy, recording or information and retrieval system without permission in writing from the publisher. For information, contact:

Hunter Halverson Press, LLC

115 West Main Street, Second Floor

Madison, WI 53703

info@hunterhalversonpress.com

{d}
Dedication

Dedicated to America's millions of water skiers – who owe so
much to Ralph Samuelson and who should listen to him now!

Gregor Ziemer
Lake City, Minnesota
1975

{ }

Dedicated to my grandfather Gregor Ziemer,
who never skied on Lake Pepin.
But, in my childhood mind, he walked on Lake Pepin.
His love has always been
my life preserver in stormy waters.

And to his great grandchild Alissa Myer
who has yet to ski on Lake Pepin.

Gail Eadie
Lake City, Minnesota
2005

{a}
Acknowledgments

The late author Gregor Ziemer acknowledges Ralph W. Samuelson for the honor of being chosen to hear and write his life story, as well as the people of Lake City who helped document the invention of water skiing.

He further acknowledges his daughter Patricia Lyon for delegating the preservation of his manuscripts to his granddaughter Gail Eadie, and he thanks his dear friend Virginia Holst for advocating that this manuscript be published.

Hunter Halverson Press, LLC, would like to further acknowledge all those who contributed to telling this story including: Constance Anderson, Georgene Arndt, Allen Bubolz, Catherine Ditmar, Gail Eadie, Harley Flathers, Robert and Florence Fick, Charlyne Wold Foss, Art Von Helmst, Herb Hinck, Carol Lowe, Carolyn McCormick, Lynn Novakofski, Phil Nyberg, Bob Parrott, Steve and Sam Roberts, Lucy Sontag, the usual morning coffee crowd at The Galley, and Virginia Holst, whose devotion to both her hometown hero Ralph W. Samuelson and long-time friend Gregor Ziemer pushed forward the publication of the manuscript.

We are additionally grateful for the research assistance provided by the American Water Ski Educational Foundation, *The Lake City Graphic*, the Lake City Chamber of Commerce, The Lake City Public Library, and the Minnesota Turkey Growers Association.

And special thank you to three essential team members whose literary and artistic contributions turn manuscripts into magic:

Karen Bankston, for an especially sharp eye and keen logic; Ann Christianson, for her artistic and graphic design work; and Rebecca Wasieleski for her talented editing and organizing, all performing brilliantly under tight time constraints.

Thank you to the intrepid newspaper reporter Margaret Crimmins whose curiosity at the Lake City boathouse in July of 1963 revealed to all of us that Ralph W. Samuelson invented water skiing.

To Ben Simons, Logan Johnson and the Lake City leaders who pushed to gain Ralph W. Samuelson and their city the recognition each truly deserved.

And, lastly, to Providence, which led Hunter Halverson Press, LLC, to publish this inspiring story.

{t}
Table of Contents

{ f }

Foreword

For decades, Gregor Ziemer's story of Ralph W. Samuelson, *Witness on Water Skis*, as originally titled, had been written and held closely by family members. Because his death was sudden and unexpected, Mr. Ziemer never had the opportunity to edit or polish the manuscript before it could be presented for publication. Therefore, we have fact checked the material with Ralph W. Samuelson contemporaries, many now in their nineties, to authenticate as much as possible the story and events presented. Also confirmed was the fact that some names in the manuscript were changed from their original to protect the privacy of relationships discussed throughout the book. These choices have been honored, as Mr. Ziemer chose to provide an honest account but one that was also respectful. The book is about the people of Lake City, Minnesota, as much as it is about the life and times of Ralph W. Samuelson.

Other editorial changes made were designed to maintain the integrity of the message and subject matter of the material while balancing those essentials with style and readability. To this extent, some material was eliminated, usually material that was duplicative of facts and events, and modifications made in organization.

Gregor Ziemer was a man that made great contributions to not only America but also to humanity, much of which will never be known or written about. We feel privileged to be chosen by the family to present to you Gregor Ziemer's manuscript, now titled *A Daredevil & Two Boards: Ralph Samuelson, The Lake Pepin Pioneer Who Invented Water Skiing*.

{ i }

Introduction

Providence dominated Ralph W. Samuelson's life and determined, according to him, his fortunes. As an eager teenager with unshakeable confidence that he could transform mundane aquaplaning into exciting water skiing just by strapping pine boards to his feet, or as an innovating turkey farmer who experienced bankruptcy, Ralph W. Samuelson anchored his life in faith. It is hard to tell which faith dominated: His faith in God or his faith in himself.

The deep waters of Lake Pepin were only an obstacle; the real challenge to his faith was the ridicule and doubt directed toward him by those who came to watch him drown. The pioneering spirit that pulled him from Lake Pepin waters July 2, 1922, and birthed a new recreation now enjoyed by millions, continued throughout his life.

Ralph W. Samuelson rose above the waves into sports history, an accomplishment that would not be recognized for decades. Not until Margaret Crimmins, a reporter possessing the same pioneering spirit, spied two forgotten pine boards bolted to a boathouse wall. She inquired, "Are those really the world's first water skis?" Her report of the exhilaration and excitement she experienced while gliding on the same pine boards used 40 years before brought Ralph W. Samuelson out of obscurity and led to the recognition he deserved, yet modestly never claimed. Providence not only led Ms. Crimmins to the boathouse that day to discover Ralph W. Samuelson, it also led the world to Lake City, Minnesota, … forever to be known as "The Birthplace of Water Skiing."

Minnesota Historical Society

The Father of Water Skiing made the world's first ski jump on July 8, 1925.

{1}

Section

1. THE LAKE

On Sunday, July 2, 1922, Lake Pepin, a 30-mile bulge of the Upper Mississippi River in southern Minnesota, lay as peaceful as a painted millpond, its green bluffs reflected on shiny blue marble.

The atmospheric disturbance that had hovered over the valley for three days, with low, gray clouds, had finally moved east, pulling in sunshiny summer weather. Temperatures were in the 80s.

About noon, a gentle northwest breeze sprang up, occasionally ruffling small patches of the lake's placid surface.

Obviously, Lake Pepin did not expect history to be made on it that day—with an event that would influence the lives of uncounted millions all over the world!

Not that Lake Pepin was afraid of history. It had been in its very vortex for centuries.

The Chippewas and the Sioux had used it as a dividing line, had fought to scalp-lifting death on it: voyageurs, explorers, pioneering priests, fur traders, soldiers, speculators, emigrants had found it a convenient—though tortuous—highway into the wilderness.

Canoes, pirogues, keelboats, stern-wheelers, side-wheelers, elegant luxury riverboats, awkward rafts—all had used it as a fluid path between the two saints, St. Louis and St. Paul, the former Pig's Eye.

Early French explorers—Radisson and Groseilliers, Daniel Du-Luth, Charles LeSueur; the British adventurer Jonathan Carver; the Italian Count Giacomo Beltrami; and Father Louis Hennepin, who named it the Lake of Tears after Sioux captured him—all knew Lake Pepin and were awed by its marching, blunt bluffs, gigantic graceful promontories, their feet in the river, ever-changing lights and colorations.

American pioneers knew it, too. Zebulon M. Pike, who bought "100,000 acres of fine land for a song"—his words meaning less than one cent an acre at the confluence of the Mississippi and the St. Peter; Josiah Snelling, who built Fort Snelling on part of that land; Governor Alexander Ramssey; John Jacob Astor's Henry Sibley, Franklin Steele, Hercules Dousman, Ramsay Crooks; the missionary William Boutwell and his half-breed wife, Hester Crooks.

Henry David Thoreau, who came to regain his health only to die of tuberculosis a year later, loved it. William Cullen Bryant, another visitor, called it one of the world's most fascinating spots. The 80-year-old Elizabeth Hamilton, widow of Alexander, came through it after meeting her son William down at Galena, Illinois, lead mines. The historian George Bancroft, and ex-President Franklin Pierce had been there, guests of a westering railroad. Abraham Lincoln's lanky cousin, Stephen Hanks, rafted on it.

But for years now nothing really historic had occurred on Lake Pepin—nothing for the history books, nothing for the archives.

Thanks to a tall, young adventurer of Swedish descent, fussing around practically all alone out there on Lake Pepin on the afternoon of July 2, 1922, that was about to change.

Like Ralph Samuelson's Viking ancestors, the young Swede was poised to help History. He was about to help write a new chapter for the venerable old Lake—precipitate it into the 20th Century with a 20th Century sport.

And he didn't even know he was doing it!

2. THE DAY

Although on this day Lake Pepin lay peaceful, as if dreaming of its past, the world was as restless as usual.

Over in Ireland, for instance, rebels were preparing a new stand against the English; snipers already ruled Dublin.

The French were still demanding a lowering of their debt to the United States, a grisly reminder of World War I.

From Berlin, Germany, came reports that the labor unions and the Socialist Party were calling for mass meetings to protest the assassination of their party's foreign minister, Emil Rathenau; while the Communists were vociferously demanding the arrest of General von Ludendorff and Field Marshall von Hindenburg. In Munich, a former corporal of the German army, now the chairman of the newly formed National Sozialistische Deutsche Arbeiter Partei, Adolf Hitler, called a special meeting of party members at their dark, dingy headquarters in the little Hotel Sterneckerbräu im Tal. Purpose? To plan an anti-Semitic article for their new newspaper, the *Voelkischer Beobachter*.

In Mexico, bandits were holding up yet another American oil company official, with demands for ransom.

The United States, too, had its worries.

That very day railway workers were calling for a national strike that would cripple the nation, dependent almost entirely on railroad transportation. Highways were still unpaved.

In Washington, the Senate had approved a 30-cent per bushel import duty on wheat, making many enemies abroad. In Elizabeth, N.J., Vice President Calvin Coolidge was droning out a speech, praising the spirit of economy in government; while 30 miles off the Jersey coast, 15 heavily laden ships, carrying $6 million worth of illegal bootleg liquor were waiting, angrily frustrated by federal prohibition agents from entering port to dispose of their precious wares in time for Fourth of July celebrations.

On that day, in New York City's Bryant Park, a decorated veteran of World War I collapsed of starvation.

And on that day, Babe Ruth slugged out three homers before 22,000 fans in Shibe Park, Philadelphia. St. Louis was leading in the American League, New York in the National.

On that day, eggs were selling for 21 cents in the city, 10 cents a dozen in the country; butter was 32 cents, bread 5 cents, pork chops 12 cents a pound. Gimbels in New York advertised shoes for $2.45 and fancy, two-piece outfits for women for $5.95.

New York City was starting a citywide test for diphtheria to avoid another epidemic; and a certain Doctor Albert F. Zahn, expert for the Navy, declared boldly that "the use of helicopters or vertical rising machines is not an impossibility."

Americans were reading a book called *Love*, in which, according to its jacket, "Andre Tridan, the author, rips the veil from love's secret taboos." It sold for $2.50.

Vance Thompson had just published his *Eat and Grow Thin*. Book Tarkington's *Gentle Julia* was selling well, and *If Winter Comes* by the English novelist A.S.M. Hutchinson was in its 365th thousand. People were devouring Ellen Glasgow, Noel Coward, William Jennings Bryan, whose *Answer to Darwin* was in its fifth edition.

And the young man out there on Lake Pepin, Ralph Samuelson, hadn't read any of them. He didn't have time.

That day, in its Sunday edition, the *New York Times* devoted 10 pages of its pictorial section to photographs of the royal wedding of King Alexander of Yugoslavia and Princess Maria of Romania.

Fanny Brice was cavorting at the Palace on New York's Broadway. The movies were presenting Wallace Reid in *The Dictator* and Jack Holt in *While Santa Sleeps*.

And on that day, something happened on Lake Pepin.

But the world wasn't interested one tiny shred in a little old Lake in a state called Minnesota.

Where was Minnesota anyway?

3. THE TOWN

On that sleepy Sunday, Lake City, the only incorporated municipality on the Minnesota shore of Lake Pepin, wasn't doing much, good or bad, worrying very little—expecting even less.

In the forenoon many of its 2,500 citizens had worshipped in the town's 13 churches. Lake City took its religion seriously—at least most of its citizens did.

Now, shortly after noon, the town was quiet. As every Sunday its 13 saloons and free lunch bars, to match the 13 churches, were closed, as were all stores. Nobody engaged in gross commercialism on the Lord's Day.

The three gas stations in town were not open for business, even though a few cars came bumping through—mostly frivolous folks from the Twin Cities, 60 miles upriver.

Lindeen's Grocery, on North Sixth, did not deliver on Sundays; Gilbertson and Rother, Ludwig's, Kemp and Roschen, Coleman's Grocery at the corner of Pearl and Main (soon to be renamed Lyon Avenue and Lakeshore Drive)—all were shut tight.

On the veranda of Hotel Lyon nearer the Lake, a few cronies were exchanging gossip, their armchairs tilted against the gray board wall.

"I hear hard times is comin'," said Hank McSweeney, retired farmer. "Eveything's goin' to pot."

"You're danged right, by golly," agreed Ollie Swenson, former railroad worker. "I hear even the price of beer's goin' up."

"Five cents a glass is too darned much already," Hank Miller, former horse shoer, joined in.

"Pretty soon they're even goin' to charge us for them free lunches they put out on the counter. That'll be the day!" growled Hank.

With that gloomy thought, they went back to dozing.

The presses of the *Lake City Graphic-Republican* and the *Waba-*

sha County Leader were inked and ready to go—come Monday.

H.A. Young Dry Goods and Clothing, corner of Lakeshore and Center, had put out special displays of summer sales, but nobody did much window shopping on Sunday either. Even Collins' Pharmacy and Drug Store wasn't open, its window displaying a big wooden bucket of horehound candy, a brown cascade on brown wrapping paper.

A few miles out in the country, beyond the railroad tracks, the hot summer sun was brooding over the young trees and flourishing shrubs and flowers of the Jewell Nursery, where tomorrow morning at seven o'clock, hundreds of boys and men would start grubbing again, at 60 cents a day. But today nobody worked.

Half a mile south, the Tennant and Hoyt Flouring Mill, famous for its Golden Loaf Flour, was shut down, too, letting its white dust settle dangerously before starting another week. The Simons Block, the Wise and Sons Block, the Lyon Street Block—everywhere locked doors, closed stores, gathering summer heat that would linger inside all week, wafted about by a few overhead electric fans.

Facing the Lake, where it was a little cooler, the Wisconsin Button Factory—which stamped round discs out of clam shells dredged up from the bottom of Lake Pepin—and its rival, the Lake Pepin Pearl Button Company, corner of Washington and Marion, were silent, although the stench of dead clams lay persistently over everything.

Mayor T.J. Foley was spending the day at Frontenac, a fashionable summer resort north of town.

The "Verana," venerable 50-foot ferry boat that crossed from Lake City to Stockholm, Wisconsin, on the far side of the 3-mile-wide Lake Pepin, lugged its heavy barge. It had just pulled out of the muddy harbor, not much more than a pond with an outlet to the lake, for its second and last run of the day—cost, 25 cents per crossing. Its smoke was low over the eastern horizon.

Now the Lake was deserted—except for that boy Ralph Samuelson and his elder brother Ben—still working at a strange, impossible, grueling, self-appointed task. A wet task.

"He's crazy all right, like everybody always says. He'll drown any minute now," growled frisky old Joe O'Malley, the town bum, fishing from a projecting boulder. "Crazy as a loon when the moon's shinin'. Crazy, that's what he is. I always said so. Crazy!"

4. THE HOUR

Lake City had, as yet, no modern bathhouse.

The beach wasn't very inviting anyway. Eventually, however, a few bold ones who had finished reading their Sunday paper or were fed up with visiting the neighbors, came down to the Lake, the women in full-bloomered bathing suits, exposing no tempting, sinful flesh except face and hands; the men in knee-length breeches, belts, knee socks, shirts with long sleeves.

Prominent among the young fry, skimming stones over the water, was 10-year-old Ben Simons, with a sharp, intelligent face, inquisitive brown eyes, strong brown hair. Lou Macklin, older, skeptical, was at Ben's side.

"That crazy 'Sammy.' He'll drown hisself," drawled Lou.

"You couldn't drown him," objected Ben, rising belligerently to the defense of a man he hero-worshipped. "He'll do it. Wait and see. He'll do it."

Nobody else bothered to watch the foolish action out on the Lake except small, blond Nancy Philips, who came running down to the half-empty beach, calling to her friend Susie, "There's that crazy Ralph Samuelson again. There he goes—like he always does—down. Let's watch him drown."

"I don't wanta see nobody drown," exclaimed Susie, shaking her yellow curls. "Let him drown. But I don't have to look."

Ben Simons paid no attention. Girls knew nothing about motorboats, and fishing, and clamming, and swimming—and big brave heroes, like Ralph Samuelson, who wasn't afraid of anything.

Ben stood and stared. Some 100 yards offshore, where the water was about 10 feet deep, the smelly old launch, getting a Sunday reprieve from dragging a clamming barge with its stinking hooks across the Lake, started its coughing Saxon truck engine once more. At top speed it would make less than 14 knots.

"Why don't he stick to his aquaplane? He's good at that," complained Lou. "Him and that Red Walstrom are good on that aquaplane board. Why don't he stick to that?"

"Because he don't want to do what everybody else can do," answered Ben. "He's got to do it on them long boards of his."

"There he goes again!" chuckled Lou. "Every time the boat starts to pull him, down he goes, right to the bottom. He must have swallowed half the Lake by now. Crazy, that's what he is."

"But look, what's he doin' now?" worried Ben. "He's swimmin' farther out with them boards. What's he doin'? He's puttin' them back on his feet. I can see 'em. The tips are stickin' out of the water."

From a greater distance, where the water was at least 20 feet deep, came the more rapid, staccato cough of the old Saxon motor again—gaining speed slowly.

Ben Simons stared, his brown eyes goggling. "Look! Look, Lou! He's doin' it! I told you he would! I told you! That boat pulled him right up and he's skiing on water. 'Sammy' is skiing on water! Like a duck just takin' off. Like a duck."

Lou spit into the sand, "Yeah, I guess he's skiing on water all right. Hope he's satisfied now."

"Hurrah, he done it! 'Sammy' done it like he always said he would!" exulted Ben, hero-worshipping with his voice and eyes! "I don't care what you say—he done it!"

"I'm goin' fishin'. Join old Joe over there. I see he's pullin' them in. As for that 'Sammy'—I don't care what he done," said Lou.

The rest of the world didn't care either—didn't give a squashed dime about what happened on Lake Pepin at that hour.

Not even Lake City cared.

The bells of St. Mary, St. Mark, St. John didn't ring; the fire whistle atop the old Georgian-style red brick city hall and fire station didn't howl; the newly organized Louis McCahill Post 110 of the American Legion didn't organize a parade. In fact, nothing happened at all.

But the truth remained: on that sleepy afternoon, July 2, 1922, at the sleepy hour of 4:11 p.m., teenager Ralph Samuelson became the first human being to ski on water.

Later—much later—the American Water Ski Association, official guardian of America's skiers, Lake City, the state of Minnesota, the nation, the world would realize—and care—very much and honor Ralph Samuelson.

But not yet. Not for 44 years!

5. THE DAREDEVIL

Did Ralph himself realize what he had done that Sunday afternoon in 1922?

Did he know he had made history—at least water ski history?

Was he aware of the forces he was helping to release?

Was he conscious of the fact that he was starting a sport, which today has millions of followers in the United States alone with millions more to come?

He was not!

To him, it was merely the fulfillment of something he started out to accomplish years before and was too stubborn to give up.

Not that he was satisfied when he finally managed to do it. He was never satisfied with his achievements. There was always something new to try, some new challenge to meet.

"Did I feel like a pioneer on that day?" he said 50 years later when, once again by the shore of Lake Pepin, near the identical spot where Ben Simons had watched him do his first successful skiing stunt, Ralph Samuelson, then 69, was interviewed for a Twin Cities television program by three teenage students from Robbinsdale, Minnesota, High School—John McCabe, Marie Davidson, and Julie Challman.

"All I felt at the time," Ralph said, reminiscing for the listeners of WCCO-TV's popular program, "Years to Youth," was that at long last I had proved to my family, to myself, and a lot of Doubting Thomases who had been laughing at me for months, calling me a silly fool, and worse, labeling me 'Nutty Sammy,' that sort of thing, that I could do what I had set out to do—ski on water, as I had skied on snow most of my life.

"Oh, sure, I did have a certain sense of elation, a certain welcome freedom. I had been aquaplaning for years, with a long, six-foot, 30-inch board, which I had modified by rounding it at both ends. But an aquaplane is tied to a boat, and has to go precisely where the boat goes. But finally, there I was, holding the rope in my hands, my feet free to go where I steered them, within limits, of course."

"When you started to ski that day, did you think you would become famous?" asked John McCabe, himself doing a bit of hero worshipping.

"No," said Ralph Samuelson emphatically. "I had no idea the sport would become so popular, or that my name would ever be known. I had no idea the thing would progress beyond myself. How could I?"

"Were you frightened by the idea of skimming along on top of the water?"

"I was just at the age when people don't frighten easily. I was an adventurer. Of course, that spirit of adventure got me into trouble at times; but it never stopped me. I think it's natural that young people of America are adventurous. That's what makes our country so great. We get ideas, and carry them out."

"What did the members of your family think of this foolhardy stunt of skimming across water behind a boat, apparently defying all laws of gravity?" asked one of the girls.

"Not only some members of my family, but lot of others insisted that skiing was for snow. But I always thought otherwise. It was the aquaplane that helped me to believe that water skiing was possible.

So now 50 nations around the world have a joyous water sport."

"Did you get rich from your invention?" he was asked. Ralph Samuelson smiled ruefully. "I never made a penny out of it. But it's sure a lot of satisfaction to know that you've created a good, clean sport for young people of today. I still devote lot of my time to teaching others to ski.

"I guess I'm a pretty humble person. I feel happiness comes from teaching others. Of course, at the time, a lot of people thought I was a little off upstairs. You know, if you have an idea and carry it through, you're sometimes considered a nonconformist. But it was my idea to ski on water, and I believed in it. If you have an idea, and think it's a good one, for the service of mankind, you should see it through against all difficulties.

"So, in my way, I was a nonconformist. So what? I'm glad I was. Maybe what we need is more nonconformists who have the guts to come out and tell people what they think and believe. I started as an 18-year-old. I haven't quit yet."

On that July 2, 1922, Ralph Samuelson was 18, with one day to spare. He would be 19 come midnight—six feet tall, straight as a Minnesota white pine, with a long Swedish profile, deep-set, ice-blue eyes, light brown hair, always meticulously parted down the middle.

According to his own description, "I was strong as an ox, a bit of a daredevil—and more than a bit of a water rat. I lived by the philosophy, 'How do you know you can't do it, until you've actually tried it?'"

6. THE SKIS

Ralph always said that he couldn't remember when he first got the idea that if you could ski on snow, why not on water?

"Maybe I'd been thinking about it ever since I was able to slide down the snowy banks of the Mississippi on barrel staves, which were our poor man's substitute for real skis," he said years later during another TV interview.

"But finally the idea nagged me so hard, that every time I went near that Lake, either to play or fish; or later when I was on it in old Zack Nihart's fishing scow, or Fred Rose's clamming outfit, I wondered—wouldn't it be great to skip along on the surface, like one of those almost transparent dragon flies that did it like magic?

"All that winter of 1921-22 I dreamt about it. When the ice finally left that spring—I think it was the first week in April—I could hardly wait to get out and see what new adventures I'd experience.

"That Lake has been a sort of mystic force in my life, ever since I can remember. I had licked it partly—had been to its bottom in deep dives, had been in it, on it in boats and aquaplanes, with ice-boats and skates. Now my hope was to glide over it—an obsession it was, almost.

"As soon as the water got a little warmer—and that doesn't happen fast in Minnesota—I began to experiment. First with the proverbial old barrel staves, I sank.

"I used snow skis, I sank.

"Finally I went to the Botsford Lumber Yard on Franklin Street, a few blocks from our home, and bought two pieces of lumber, eight feet long, nine inches wide—plain pine boards, really, ½-inch thick. A fellow called Giorges sold them to me for $1 each.

"I took them home, dipped the tips in mother's old copper wash boiler, the kind people use for antique planters now, and boiled them for three hours or longer—like dirty shirts.

"In the tool shed back of our little white house I still had the forms I used to mold my aquaplane—vises and clamps and braces. I put the two pieces of wood in those vises, left them there for two full days. My sister, Harriet, and my brother, Ben, both older than myself, helped."

Harriet recalled that day when her brother created his first water skis—in fact, the world's first.

"Ralph often had ideas nobody else would have dared to have. He is two years younger than me and, of course, girls just weren't included in most of my brother's fun. But we all helped him to build something we never dreamed would become what it is today. I can remember vividly helping him hold the ends of those clumsy boards in mother's wash boiler, filled with water heated on our old iron kitchen range, and pumped out of our cistern by means of the old kitchen pump. Ralph was what we would call a daredevil. Nothing much stopped him! At least we couldn't."

After two days in the crude vise, the boards had permanently bent tips.

"Harriet and I put a coat of white paint on them, to help pre-serve the wood," Ralph recalled. "At Henry Baesler's Harness Shop, on South Washington, I bought two narrow leather straps—rather, they gave me some scrap leather. I fastened them on the boards, about halfway down, with wood screws.

"Then I rushed to Ruechert's Hardware Store and bought 100 feet of sash cord. At Pearson's Blacksmith Shop, on the corner of Chestnut and Washington, where the shoeing of horses was still big business, I pestered them until they made me an iron ring, about four inches in diameter. I wrapped that with black insulation tape, to make it easier on my hands and tied it to the end of the line.

"We attached the sash cord to the back of my brother's smelly, slow boat, and he got her going. We were in fairly shallow water, but deep enough to swim in. Somehow I got those heavy skis attached to my bare feet, my brother accelerated—and down I went to the bottom of Lake Pepin, into the slime and mud with the clams.

"That was on Wednesday, June 28. I had had enough for that day. And, I confess, that evening word got around among my friends, and they sure had a laugh at my expense. But they'd been calling me a crazy dreamer so long, one more laugh didn't matter—much.

"The next day the Lake was still calm, although it was a cloudy day. I used a different technique. I fastened my aquaplane behind the boat, got on it, carrying the monstrous skis. After we got go-ing, I put the skis on. It was tricky, but I had been stunting on that aquaplane so long, riding on Red Walstrom's shoulders, standing on my head on a backless chair, and all, that I managed.

"I stepped off the aquaplane with my skis on—one foot at a time—and sure enough, I slid along the surface of the water, even ventured a few yards away from the bouncing aquaplane.

"I suppose, in a way, that was the beginning of water skiing. But I felt strongly that until I had found a way to start on those things, I wasn't really doing it right.

"We tried the aquaplane-to-ski transfer for several days. And then, somehow, from somewhere, came a thought. I'd been holding the tips of my skis on the level or downward when I started.

"What if I'd start with them out of the water, slanting upward?"

7. THE BEGINNING

"Then on Sunday, July 2, it happened," Samuelson remembered, his eyes a little filmy. "I hadn't been to church. Never went to church in those days. What for?

"We were in deeper water. I managed to keep afloat, squatting, with the tips of those giant skis out of the water.

"And sure enough, when Brother Ben gave his stinking old tub all the juice she had, up I came—like that goddess, what's her name, who came out of the waves. And away we went.

"I had done it!

"I was skiing on water!!

"Had I realized what I had started, perhaps I would immediately have patented my skis—gotten some sort of publicity, had myself photographed by sports magazines, perhaps had cards printed, calling myself "The Inventor of Water Skiing"—cashed in somehow. God knows we needed the money.

"Why didn't I?

"I hate to admit it, but I guess I wasn't as smart then as I should have been. Fact is, I was stupid about the significance of what I had done. Don't believe me if you don't want to, but the sad truth is, I never made a wooden nickel out of the whole blessed idea—not an Indian head penny.

"But as I told some kids who interviewed me, I've had other rewards—big rewards. And I now know something I didn't know then. That very moment, at 4:11 p.m., July 2, 1922, the good Lord chose me for a mission, a mission I am finally—after more than 50 years of delay—fulfilling. This is not my story. It's God's story!"

If God was aware of Ralph Samuelson on that July day in 1922, when he first skimmed along Lake Pepin's still clean surface, on his gigantic skis, He didn't indicate it in any way.

The people who actually saw him perform his feat soon forgot about Ralph Samuelson.

Oh, they remembered him for a year or so. Then they blanked him out of their memories.

The weekly *Lake City Graphic-Republican* in its annual summary of the important events of the year 1922, the year when Samuelson water skied for the first time, stated that it was the mildest winter in history. It reported a serious accident that happened in a steam-planing factory in town, when a boy named Eddie Collins lost a hand in a planer.

But it did not mention a boy named Ralph Samuelson. His invention, or whatever it could have been called, received no publicity whatsoever.

That event just wasn't news in the eyes of the town's leading paper.

But eventually it became news—national news.

{2}

Section

8. THE MIDWIFE

Two score and four years after his first successful water skiing event, Ralph Samuelson was finally beginning to be recognized by the American Water Ski Association as the bonafide Father of Water Skiing. He was written up in many magazines and newspapers, including the official publication of the association, *The Water Skier*.

None gave any background to Samuelson's life.

Why?

The answer lies partly in the fact that Ralph himself never said much about his early childhood.

But his background is colorful, picturesque, molded by the pioneering spirit of an indomitable pioneer family. Nor was that family exactly typical.

It was shortly after midnight, July 2, 1903. Mrs. Oscar—Isabelle—Peterson, more familiarly known as "Laundry" Peterson, the midwife who was called into frenzied service by most members of the Swedish and German community in Lake City on certain occasions, was waddling down what she still called Pearl Street, turned north on Main, then hurried one block over to the corner of Washington and Doughty.

One of those streets was obviously named after the father of his country; the other, after Samuel Doughty, who, together with Abner Dwelle and Abner Tibbits, was a pioneer of Lake City, back in the 1850s and 1860s.

One of Doughty's sons, J. Cole, still lived in the magnificent Doughty mansion on Doughty Street, a few blocks up from the modest Samuelson home. The historic old building eventually had to give way for the Lake City Woman's Club.

J. Cole was associated with the Jewell Nursery, where young Ralph pulled weeds as soon as he was old enough to tell a dandelion from a daisy. A brother, Frank Doughty, who had lost an arm in a flouring mill, was a prominent citizen, and a justice of the peace. Another Doughty, John, once owned a sloop-rigged sailboat named "Union," used for ferry service across Lake Pepin, an early forerunner of the "Verana," which Ralph later encountered when he was swimming the harbor, in the nude...

"Laundry," comfortably plump, always carried her white enameled dishpan, a rather cold catchall for babies and one of the few tools she ever used in her trade; and her little black bag with bedroom slippers, towels, extra diapers, smelling salts for the new mother, some rubbing alcohol, and cornstarch to be used as baby powder.

She had been to the Charles and Mary Samuelson home before. "Laundry" tried to remember—first it had been Ben, some eight years ago; Clarence, two years later—the poor kid had died at the age of 2, victim of that horrible thing, diphtheria. Then came a girl, Harriet, now 2 years old.

"Laundry" wondered, vaguely, as she hurried through the completely deserted, unpaved streets, how the Samuelsons managed to space them that way—every two years or so? Maybe they had some sort of system?

"Laundry" didn't know how many yelling brats she had helped to enter this miserable vale of tears. Some of her clients had one every year.

Charles Samuelson, who owned a grocery store at 102 E. Center Street in the heart of town, had paid his $2.50 for the delivery of each of his three previous kids promptly. He probably would pay this bill too.

"Laundry" waddled a little faster. Eight-year-old Ben had come running an hour ago, scared of the dark, but acting brave, blurting out his mother wanted her to come quick.

Usually in these births there were several false alarms. But you could never tell. Mary had always had normal births. This was her fourth. No problems, probably.

Someday, perhaps, there would be a hospital in town for the complicated cases. There was talk even now of buying some private home for the purpose—maybe that big white house of Senator Greer. As it was, sick people, or those who ended up with problems after childbirth, had a choice: die idle at home or go to one of the two practical nurses in town, Mrs. Mary Kopp, or Mrs. Christine Lamb. The dear ladies often did the impossible. Often they were helpless.

Of course, as long as the municipality had "Laundry" Peterson, babies would make it into the sinful world—if the parents had done their share and started healthy ones.

Ralph Samuelson arrived without too much fuss, slapped into his first yell, and washed in the white dishpan. In the early dawn of July 3, 1903, he was born in the big bedroom on the lower floor, north side, of the small white frame house, with its two-holer backhouse (where later stood a boathouse), its back porch with the tall red pump, a kitchen with its old cast-iron range, a 20-by-24-foot family living room, where most of the family living was done, especially in winter, which sometimes meant seven months.

Of course, the living room was off limits while mother was having another baby. That left the 16-by-16-foot dining room, with the big pull-out pine table, always willing to accept whatever food the occasion could muster—sometimes much, sometimes little.

Said Ralph's only sister, Harriet, "Ralph was an average baby, and an average boy. Maybe he was pampered a little. Later, when he joined our table, he sometimes got by with leaving a bit of food on the plate when we were told to clear ours. Food was never wasted in our house.

"Looking back, I really think he was mother's favorite. At least he knew just how to get around her and get his way—many times. But that didn't stop her from teaching us all right from wrong, as many of the old Swedish parents did. Wish we had more like her today!"

9. THE MOTHER

Whenever Ralph Samuelson talked of his mother, he usually added, with a touch of pride, "She was Swedish, you know!"

She certainly was—through and through.

Born in Värmland, southern Sweden, Mary Larson came to her chosen land, as she always called it, in 1887 with a group of intrepid pioneers. She was 16.

Her ocean liner was a cattle boat, the kind used by so many Swedish emigrants.

As often happened, her party was accompanied by a minister of the gospel and his wife. The good pastor did his best to keep his flock in good spirits.

As many other emigrants, Mary lived first with relatives in a small settlement along one of the many swampy inlets of the Mississippi, on the Wisconsin side opposite Lake City—already a busy farming community, with five saloons, and five churches. The town had a future, for it was attached to the outer world by a double-stranded umbilical cord, a railroad.

Like other Wisconsin girls of her hamlet—first known as Shoo Fly, and then, without improving itself much, renamed Bogus Creek—Mary Larson made a bold move and ferried across the water to Lake City, which had more job opportunities.

She found work with a family named Woodford.

One Sunday, while visiting with her folks back home, Mary met a farmer's son—Charles Samuelson—who worked his father's acres up on the Wisconsin plateau near Lund, a pioneer settlement sprawling around a substantial brick church.

Charles wanted to get away from that farm. It was too lonesome for his convivial nature.

They were married in 1894, he age 24 (born in Chicago, said the marriage application); she age 23.

They settled in Lake City. Charles had noble dreams of becoming somebody important. He never quite made it: his grocery store went bankrupt, eventually; he didn't live long enough to see his son become famous, either.

The Samuelsons changed addresses several times, according to the records, ending up at 317 N. Washington, where Ralph was born, where he grew up.

If any Superior Power governed his life as he progressed from the burping stage to a toddler and a runner-around, it may have been personified in his older brother, Ben, who watched over him. In turn, Ralph was older brother to Donald, two years younger, and to Charles.

As far as anybody could tell, God didn't seem too interested in the Samuelsons. And they certainly weren't too interested in Him. They were what was known as "God-fearing, but not pious."

Although exposed to some religion, Ralph didn't absorb any, partly because it was administered in Swedish, a language he couldn't understand. He couldn't read the Swedish Bible, couldn't comprehend a word of the thundering Swedish sermons bellowed out by the old, long-bearded Reverend Peterson at the small Swedish Mission Church at Sixth and Walnut.

Nor did he appreciate the songs of the small choir, reinforced occasionally with a twanging guitar or the blare of a cornet.

Said Ralph, "Almost all I remember of my early contact with church was that the leader of the small group, who often became an emergency soloist, was an old maid, fat, off-tune, with a black ribbon partly covering her large goiter. It was fascinating to watch that ribbon bob up and down as she sang.

"At Christmas time the children, including me, were given small, red and white striped bags of candy. The Christmas tree, a real fir from the woods or the Jewell Nursery, once caught fire from the wax candles stuck into metal candle holders welded onto three circular bands of iron. That fire was more exciting than getting presents.

"At Easter time each child received an Easter egg—a hard-boiled hen's egg. I gobbled mine up on the way home. We always walked, of course."

Ralph had a few other memories—none of them pious.

For one thing, the Reverend John Peterson, a devout servant of God, believed that the morals of his congregation were his personal responsibility. He often spent two hours sermonizing against the eight saloons in town (their number was going up), the short skirts (almost an inch above the ankles), and especially the gambling in town.

Some of this "gambling" was going on in a so-called "sinners' nest," right on the shore of historic Lake Pepin. It was not a nightclub or a casino or a house of ill fame run by a sinful madam. It was only a shack, a warming house for iceboat devotees. Ice boating, racing along on one of those slender frames on wide-spaced runners, equipped with huge rails, while lying on your stomach, only a few inches from the ice, was one of the popular—and dangerous—sports on Lake Pepin in winter. It was long before the days of noisy snowmobiles.

Sometimes, when the ice was smooth and the wind strong, an iceboat could develop speeds up to 100 miles an hour.

The gambling that aroused the Reverend Peterson's shouting fury was card playing in this old pine board shack, heated by a pot-bellied Franklin stove.

One Sunday, he preached so convincingly against this den of evil that the ladies of the congregation became hysterically convinced vice was taking over the whole community.

They formed a mob that Sunday night, much to the disgust of levelheaded Mary Samuelson, and set fire to the little old shanty by the shore of the Lake, burning the poor thing to the frozen ground.

It was never rebuilt. Nobody dared.

While adult Swedes listened attentively to the preacher's hell-and-damnation tirade, some of the younger boys, including Ralph and his good friend, Vernie Johnson, who later became a pillar of the community and a well-known executive of the Jewell Nursery, were restless.

They played a game to pass the hours.

The low ceiling was made of ornamental, corrugated metal, stamped and molded to resemble fancy, square blocks.

The boys spent several sermons counting and recounting those blocks—and comparing notes at post-church coffee-drinking time, to see if they agreed.

After the third Sunday they both came up with the same number, 292. The Reverend Peterson probably thought the little angels were reverently elevating their eyes toward Heaven in prayer while they were doing their counting.

Of the two, Vernie was apparently the more restless. He finally brought along a very unholy bean shooter. While the Reverend Peterson was lambasting sinners, threatening the fires of eternal damnation for each and every one of them, Vernie, obviously a deadly shot, landed a sinful white bean directly on the preacher's large, holy Swedish nose.

Had the good man of God been a more tolerant man, he would probably have controlled his temper, possibly turned the other cheek, as his Boss upstairs demanded.

This pastor wasn't that kind of man. He leaped down from the pulpit, and in two mighty jumps reached Vernie's pew, hit the lad over the head with his heavy Bible and knocked him right out of his seat.

There might have been murder in the aisle hadn't Vernie's more pious sister, Norma, alarmed, scared, and quick, yanked him out of the door to go scurrying home.

That was probably the last time Vernie went to that church. Ralph, too, refused to go, out of sympathy for his friend—and out of fright.

It didn't much matter anyway. Shortly thereafter the church had to close because the congregation couldn't even pay the janitor or buy coal for the cracked old stove, much less pay the preacher.

The building later became the house of worship for the Assembly of God.

Ralph's parents never joined another church. Neither did Ralph—until "God was ready for me," as he put it later.

In fact, he attached special significance to the fact that he never went to Sunday school, never read the Bible, never heard, or at least never understood, any sermons, or even learned the ubiquitous catechism.

"God wanted to teach me the rudiments of true religion later in life. Being a religionist, attending a church, learning wordy definitions in a catechism doesn't make a disciple."

But if not religion, there obviously was one great driving force, a mysterious natural power, that did influence young Ralph's life.

It was the Lake!

10. THE BOY

To Ralph Samuelson, the Lake, which he wrote with a capital "L" his entire life, was a God-like thing.

"God worked through the Lake," Ralph insisted. "He drew me to it as if it were a big, glistening magnet, 30 miles long and three wide. Like Mark Twain's Tom Sawyer and Huckleberry Finn, "I was held by that Lake as if it had fingers around both of my wrists.

"I'm positive, if it hadn't been for my intimacy with Lake Pepin, I would never have had the stamina, the fearlessness, and the foolhardy notion to swim in it, pull fish and clams out of it, aquaplane on it—and eventually conquer it with my skis.

"All very corny? But in my opinion about as corny as my majestic Lake, bordered with majestic bluffs and hills, with deep cuts made by coulees.

"I've seen that Lake rear up in anger, and I've seen it lie docile and innocent like the blanket over a baby—a blue blanket. But, always, it was God's challenge to me, to come and conquer it.

"And conquer it I did. It aroused in me a spirit of adventure that stayed with me all my life. I still have it. Only those raised from birth by the shore of a Lake like Pepin will fully understand what I mean, I guess."

This conquest of Lake Pepin began almost before Ralph could walk. "Most of us can remember the first really big thing that happened to us—sometimes good, sometimes bad, sometimes painful," said Ralph.

"The first memory I have, is that of running away to the Lake—it was mostly downhill, only two blocks or so—and standing on the brink of what seemed a gigantic drop-off near an old cottonwood tree. There I stood and watched a big side-wheeler push a large raft of logs, 100 feet long and 300 wide, to some downriver sawmill. To me that was mystery, romance, glory—adventure. To be on that raft and go floating along, on the water—oh, that would be happiness.

"Another memory I have is that of the packets "Cyclone" and "Red Wing" meeting in midstream, saluting each other with their melodious whistles; and the "Morning Star," which made regular trips up and downriver, stopping to take on passengers.

"I'd just stand there, my eyes glassy, dreaming how thrilling it would be to ride on one of those boats. It was almost as if I had a yearning to be part of that Old Mississippi and its bulge, Lake Pepin. It seeped into my blood, that wish, that hunger. And it stayed with me. And as I grew, the hunger grew, until it almost devoured me.

"That river bank soon became a playground for me, where I could find a hundred things to do."

But in the early days of the century many residents of Lake City, as well as those of Red Wing upriver and Reed's Landing, Wabasha and Winona downriver, were afraid of Lake Pepin. Including Mary Samuelson. To them, Lake Pepin was a monster, a killer.

That phobia dated back to a catastrophe. The whole valley was still under its shadow, although it had happened 13 years before Ralph was born.

Some residents of Lake Pepin towns would not go out on that Lake, at any price.

It was called by local historians "the worst disaster that ever blighted the Upper Mississippi," and possibly the worst, save one, on the entire river in number of lives lost. It occurred about two miles off shore, near Central Point, a promontory of land just north of Lake City. That was the capsizing of the little steamer "Sea Wing" in a cyclonic storm on the night of July 13, 1890, when 98 men, women and children met death.

The "Sea Wing" had brought a full load of happy sightseers and excursionists to Camp Lakeview below Lake City, where the Minnesota National Guard went for annual summer training and maneuvers.

The steamer was only 110 tons, flat-bottomed, with twin

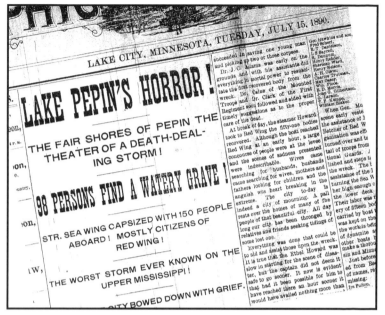

Lake City Graphic.

stacks, and main, boiler, and roof decks, and had a barge called "Jim Grand" lashed to her side. She was on her way back to Red Wing from the camp, again heavily loaded, when the storm struck, after a blistering, hot day. Somebody got panicky, cut loose the stabilizing barge, unbalancing the pitching ship. It turned completely over.

Her machinery tore loose, and ripped through the upside-down roof. Then the ship righted herself, and the passengers, many of whom had managed to crawl on her hull, were thrown back into the water. All the women and children, who had fled inside to the ladies' cabin, drowned there.

Ever after, Lake Pepin was designated as treacherous and unpredictable, a judgment wholly unearned and decidedly unfair, according to modern ship owners, running their yachts, cruisers, rowboats, and sailboats on the Lake today.

But it wasn't until more than half a century after the accident that the Chamber of Commerce of Lake City finally succeeded in removing an official bronze plaque—placed by the government at an observation point on the lower end of the Lake—warning against "treacherous Lake Pepin."

Nobody was happier than Ralph Samuelson when that sign disappeared from the shore of his beloved Lake one dark night.

To him Lake Pepin was a dear comrade, not a traitor to be feared!

II. THE SWIMMER

Certainly the "Sea Wing" disaster must have shocked Ralph's future mother, Mary Larson, working as a servant for the Woodford family at the time.

That fear was undoubtedly still with her when Ralph was old enough to play by, on, in, under the Lake.

Her fear made her inventive. She took a clothesline, similar to the one Ralph later used in some of his water skiing adventures, tied one end to the old cottonwood, the other securely around the waists of Ben, Ralph, Donald, and Charles.

It actually worked—for two days. On the third, it worked too well.

Ben, a monkey apparently, managed to climb up a small maple tree—to the first crotch. There he lost his hold, plummeted down the other side, and hung, dangling, screaming like a rabbit booby-trapped by a snare.

Some adult passerby cut him down.

Mary gave up that invention.

She tried a different tactic. She'd teach her water-mad kids how to swim—then perhaps she'd be able to do her washing and ironing, and cleaning and cooking and weaving in peace.

The old clothesline found a new mission.

Once again it was tied around the boys' waists. They were allowed to go out into the water as far as the rope would reach; then Mary hauled them back.

It was like being hitched to a boat while riding on an aquaplane. Ralph could go only as far as the rope permitted.

One day, as a special privilege, Mary let Ralph go down to the Lake to hunt for shells. He promised not to go into the water and intended to keep his promise.

Ralph's search took him a little upriver, to a place of mystery, often admired from a distance: a rickety pier built by an old river rat with a handicap, Walt Anderson. He used it to tie up rowboats, which he rented out to prospective city-slicker fishermen from the Twin Cities.

Ralph got up on the pier, carefully straddling the wide cracks between the narrow boards. He inspected the ropes holding the boats, couldn't resist the temptation, untied one, and watched the released boat swing slowly and begin an uncertain journey downriver.

He hadn't checked the small boathouse on shore, where the owner had been snoozing—not soundly enough.

In spite of his dragging leg, Walt Anderson could move fast, and did.

"I told you kids to stay off my dock!" he croaked, punctuating his fury with Swedish profanity, directed at the young pirate who dared to invade his moored fleet. "This time I gotcha."

Ralph saw danger coming, tried to dodge it.

"No you don't, you little brat. Who are you?" yelled Walt, glowering at the spindly, cornered boy. "Aha! I thought so. One of them Samuelsons. This time I'll teach you a lesson you ain't gonna forget."

"What you gonna do?" quavered Ralph. "I ain't done nothin'."

"Ain't done nothin'? Ain't done nothin'! Look out there! Untied my boat, didn't you?"

Walt approached warily, caught the dodging lad by the hair and the seat of his pants.

"What you gonna do?" yelled Ralph.

"Throw you in. You like boats good enough to steal one, go in after it!"

He began to swing the frightened boy, ready to toss him off the dock.

"I can't swim, I can't swim!" shrieked Ralph.

Whether it was too late to stop, or whether old Walt didn't hear, he hurled his captive far out in a screaming arc.

Ralph landed with a fearful splash, swallowed water. The Lake was much too deep to wade. There was no protective rope around his waist, no strong mother on the other end to pull him in.

He did what he had to do.

He swam.

"I remember it as if it was day before yesterday," said Ralph. "After the first shock, I realized it was natural for me to swim. It sure wasn't a fancy crawl, or a rhythmic breaststroke. It was obviously a dog paddle. But it worked."

Walt Andersen, his anger evaporated, was watching anxiously, afraid his victim was actually drowning, in which case he couldn't have saved him, handicapped as he was.

Ralph didn't drown. He made it to shore, beat it for home.

The story has a postscript.

Like a boy with a new pet, "I had to show off my newest skill," Ralph recalls. "The next day mother tied me to a clothesline again, but I managed to untie it in the water. About 400 feet out, a trim little craft called "Black Beauty" was riding at anchor. I paddled directly for it, while on shore mother let out loud bellows of anger and fear.

"I not only managed to get to the "Black Beauty," which was unoccupied, thank goodness; but I crawled on board, ran to the bow, and dove off—in a spattering belly flop.

"And I swam back to shore. When I got there, tired but beaming, mother was so glad to see me alive, she forgot to spank me, as I deserved."

That was the next step in a love affair with Lake Pepin, which never ended. That affair became so intense that Ralph Samuelson often dared to go out in weather, which cowed everybody else.

As Ralph said six decades later, when the world began to honor him as the Father of Water Skiing, "The Good Lord must have kept His eye on me. I never got hurt—as long as I was on the water."

He did get hurt, plenty, off the water, however.

Ralph went through the tribulation of being 6, then 7. Every day he could, he spent on the Lake, in winter ice boating pushed by a huge sail his mother had made, skating on a cleared spot, sleighing across with the family; in summer, fishing with his father, especially on Sundays—rowing and swimming.

What became a modern marina in Lake City was a pond, with a narrow outlet to the Lake, where in spring, when the ice broke up, huge floes would be pushed in by the north wind, later that entrance was shifted to the south side.

But north entrance or south entrance, to Ralph and his pals, it was still the old swimming hole. They took to it daily, weather permitting.

Whenever the ferry "Verana" pulled in, or pulled out, the gang simply ducked under water—until the intruder had passed. Good reason. They were all swimming in the nude. Who could afford bathing suits?

School?

Not important.

Ralph, later an articulate speaker who took a Dale Carnegie public speaking course and who was often interviewed on radio and television, never could remember much about the first four years of his schooling in the old red brick Washington Elementary on Doughty Street, later condemned; and the four years more at Lincoln, at that time almost on the edge of town, later the center of education for a whole district.

He did remember sliding down a long banister and catching pigeons that used to roost under the eaves of the brick building.

They could be reached via a fire escape and captured in nets. He also remembered some of the sleigh rides, when the whole class would go out in a box sled rented from Foley's livery stable.

He recalled the strict discipline, reinforced with taps on the knuckles with a bit of rubber hose; the treatment accorded to a friend whose clothes smelled of cigarette smoke and who was sent home; the shock he gave the class when he came in smelling decidedly of skunk, for he ran a trap line up near Sugar Loaf Bluff to earn money for school clothes and had that morning apprehended several of the black and white creatures.

He, too, was sent home—fast.

He had to burn his pants. But there was still profit in the deal. A new pair cost a quarter; but the pelts brought in 50 cents.

Later Ralph's Lake was to become not only a playground, but a work arena.

And a setting for History ...

12. THE PULLER OF WEEDS

Before Ralph was allowed to earn money on his Lake, like a man, he had to go through a phase many boys of Lake City had to experience—pulling weeds at the Jewell Nursery, one of the bigger industries of town, if not the state, 1,000 beautiful acres of young trees, shrubs, flowers, both annuals and perennials.

The schedule was strict: six days a week, 10 hours a day; pay, 60 cents a day.

For that 60 cents you crawled on your knees between rows of saplings, or you hacked away at weeds with a hoe that insisted on becoming dull.

Some days you found yourself loosening loam around apple seedlings—Grimes Golden, Jonathans, especially Wealthy, a hardy apple introduced into the cold Minnesota climate by Peter Gideon, pioneer horticulturist, who named it after his wife—or around Smedlar maples, or white birches, or linden trees.

The next day you'd be grubbing out quack grass, purple thistles, prickly horse nettles, deep-rooted knapweed, sour dock with long, tobacco-like leaves, red sorrel, and the morning glory-like bindweed that kept crawling up the young Lombardy poplars, which the nursery was raising in large fields since they had proved to be especially hardy for North and South Dakota.

A third day you could be assigned to animated, scholarly Eric Wilson and his perennial section, where you crept along and carefully pulled tough, tall teasel weeds or wild carrots, the seed of which could lie dormant in the ground for seven years.

You removed witch's grass from around columbines, Iceland poppies, meadow rues, iris, peonies, delphiniums, clematis, buddleia, rudbeckia, scabiosa, phlox, dahlias, alyssum, chrysanthemums, and the annuals, like marigolds, petunias, zinnias, snapdragons, portulaca, and bluebells.

Ralph's lifelong love for gardening and flowers had its roots in that section of the Jewell Nursery. He hated weeds then, he hated them ever since, but he loved flowers, and knew a hundred of them by name.

He hated weeding, but he needed that 60 cents a day he earned pulling them. Not that he got to keep the money. Most of it went to buy shoes, or shirts, or paper and pencils for school.

From that period, when Ralph felt uncomfortably earth-bound, came another memory—that of old John Nordine, the overseer, who sported an old Buick and lumbered back and forth across the huge plantation checking on the hired help.

Nordine, like most overseers the world over, became the subject of dislike. The Lake City gang revealed it in a song, composed by his slow-working boys:

Here comes John Nordine
With his threshing machine.

Later, when Ralph's life took a drastically religious turn, he realized painfully that he had been somewhat of a sinner in his youth. Whether this bit of poetry, which drove old Nordine to use choice cuss words because "them brats down in them weeds made a joke of him," could be labeled a sin or not, Ralph never decided.

He must have had a sense of humor even then, although it was never a boisterous one, or he would not have remembered something else about overseer Nordine.

At times, the old Swede was funny without intending to be.

During the hot summer days, all workers drank out of the same, communal water jug, everybody simply wiping the mouthpiece with a grimy finger before taking a swig.

One day, John scolded one of the gang, embellishing his speech with Swedish invectives. His target was an older man. Ralph imitated old Nordine well, spluttering as he used to:

"You old fool baan in this kountree forty-fem year, and you cain't even say yug."

The boys made up a new verses:

Here comes John Nordine
With his threshing machine.
He scalds old Nig
Who can't say jug.
And takes a swig
Out of his yug.

The nursery held Ralph prisoner during several glorious summers, until he was 10. Then he no longer had to stare at his distant Lake through shimmering summer heat, longing for its coolness, its unpredictable moods, its secrets.

He was offered a summer job with Fred Rose.

And Ralph Samuelson, future Father of Water Skiing, became a clammer on Lake Pepin.

13. THE CLAMMER

Of all the historic eras Lake Pepin has gone through, that of being the home of millions of clams was the messiest.

Once upon a time, literally hundreds of clamming boats dredged Lake Pepin's muddy bottom for clams, for it seemed the whole floor was covered with these bivalves, waiting to be harvested.

Fred Rose, tall, sparse, a typical clammer, dressed in overalls, or when the weather was rough, in Mackinaw or raincoat, was a hard-working boss and a strict disciplinarian who set a powerful example for his workers.

His particular outfit included two boats, one with a small motor, the other just a flat-bottomed skiff, each about 24 feet long. The skiff was pulled by the motorboat not prow forward, but sideways, like a scow that had lost its sense of direction.

That barge was outfitted weirdly with clamming contraptions, most important of which were the clam bars—two 3/4 inch galvanized pipes, 16 feet long, suspended between two heavy wooden braces, which could be raised and lowered with a windlass.

Each of these metal pipes carried 30 to 40 chains, about 24 inches long. At the end of each chain dangled three four-pronged clam hooks of No. 12 galvanized wire, each hook resembling a crow's foot, with sharp, pointed claws.

Clams are lazy. They spend their lives lying around, their shells wide open, waiting for the river to bring them food and carry away their waste. Comes something that bothers them, like a stick or some predator, and they shut their shells.

That's the secret of clamming.

Fred Rose, like thousands of other clammers, tossed his bars overboard, and let their 360 to 480 hooks drag along the muddy river bottom.

If one so much as touched the inside rim of a clam, the beast snapped its house shut, and kept it shut, ostensibly feeling very secure.

But once that clam had clamped its pearly mouth over that bit of metal, its life in the river was over.

The two bars kept working as a team—one would be pulled up, while the other went down, in endless repetition.

And it was Ralph's job to yank those stubborn clams, their shells still shut, off the hooks as fast as he could, before the other bar came up.

Those shells clattered like rocks when they hit the bottom of the old barge. Ralph was always barefoot. Why ruin shoes? And until his feet became tougher than a violin player's fingertips, he got many a cut.

How many millions of clams were pulled out of Lake Pepin over the years, by those searching hooks, nobody would ever try to estimate. But tons upon tons of mother-of-pearl, the fine white, shiny material under the drab, almost black covers of the clams were delivered to the two button factories of Lake City. And that town was only one of the many button centers that proliferated up and down the river.

But the shells of Lake Pepin were especially famous, for they were almost pure calcium carbonate.

For Ralph, it was a rough routine, especially when the Lake was choppy. But since it seemed the clams bit best when there was rough water, and when the river was high, old Fred Rose insisted on going out even when the hardy "Verana" hesitated to make its ferry run over to Stockholm, Wisconsin.

Rose always started early, sometimes at four in the morning, dredging up and down the Lake; he'd not come in until noon, unload the rocky freight—then go out again until dark.

And dark in that northern latitude in summer didn't happen until ten o'clock.

Little did Ralph realize that some years later he, his father, and brothers would be running their own clamming business, with all the joys, tribulations, problems—and rewards, thereof. And little did he anticipate being the first man to ski on his Lake.

It was during the second summer of working for Fred Rose that young Ralph first became aware of problems at home.

There had always been intimacy in the Samuelson home, and

much family empathy. But now, 1913, the atmosphere around the big dining table, with the clean, checkered red and white table-cloth, was often strained.

Mary, in her prime at 42, had circles under her blue eyes; 18-year-old Ben, the oldest, was out looking for work, at a time when work was scarce. He didn't want to go as far as Minneapolis.

There was talk that Rochester, about 30 miles south, with its Mayo Clinic, might some day attract industry, but so far it hadn't.

Harriet, age 12, was helping all she could.

Ralph, 10, sensitive to moods in the home, realized something was wrong.

But not until his father actually lost his grocery store on Center Street, did he realize fully how deep the family trouble was.

Charles Samuelson was a convivial, friendly man—too friendly. It was said that he bought too many drinks for too many drummers, and for too many of his customers.

As Ralph put it decades later: "You can't live long and keep a large family without doing something to earn money, so father thought he could start in the clamming business. From his bankruptcy proceedings, he had salvaged a nice launch with enough power to pull a clamming barge. So Fred Rose, the man I worked for, helped my dad get started; showed him how to make hooks, where to dredge, what to do with the clams. And with my previous experience, I became a great help to my father."

It worked out well enough, especially since the whole family joined in like veterans.

Once the barge was loaded with clams and was deep in the water, it was pulled to shore, to a spot where the Samuelsons had set up their large steam boiler, an iron container about eight feet long and three feet wide.

A wood fire was built under it, and the clams were steamed until they let go their shells forever. This separation of the clams from the homes they had built for themselves was performed on a large bench. Ralph's mother and sister did that.

The shells were tossed on a big pile that grew until it contained tons of the precious, prospective buttons.

The oozing meat was worked over by hand—in a search for pearls or slugs.

And the two women actually did find pearls. Mary discovered one so well rounded, she got $400 for it. She promptly deposited it in her own personal savings account.

The slugs, imperfectly formed blobs of mother-of-pearl, were sold by the ounce and used for odd-shaped pieces of jewelry.

But the real money lay in the shells, which were loaded on a box wagon and hauled to whichever pearl factory of the two Lake City plants offered the better price, usually about $40 to $50 a ton.

The clamming business was a success, thanks primarily to Mary, who supplied the necessary working capital.

Back in Sweden she had learned weaving. Now she searched for, found, and bought a small second-hand loom. And from then on, for many years, the "swish-swish" of the shuttle, hurled from side to side between the two sets of warp threads, alternately raised and lowered by the heddle; the "thump-thump" of the comb-like reed, as the thread was beaten against the already finished fabric; and the rattle of the shifting heddle, reversing the position of the two sets of warp, binding the weft into the fabric, could be heard day and night in the old house on Washington Street.

Mary was soon known all over town, and far beyond, as the best weaver of carpets, rugs, fancy cloth, shawls, even sails.

Ralph always knew his mother earned more than the rest of them did clamming. She sometimes turned out 10 yards of colorful, multi-patterned carpet in a day.

The heavy wooden loom took up a lot of space in the living room, the warmest room in the house, with its coal stove along the south wall. But everybody adjusted eagerly.

Ralph acquired one important, even magnificent, fringe benefit, a blessing considering what the future had in store during these years of clamming.

Said Ralph later: "While working with my father every day on Lake Pepin, we would get caught in many a bad storm, which came up suddenly. Then we had to fight our way home through big waves, at least they looked big to me from the bottom of the flat barge.

"More and more, as the weeks and months rolled by, did I feel myself become part of Lake Pepin. I could almost hear her calling me, taking me into her confidence, warning me when things got really bad, and comforting me, too.

"During that time I had to master my Lake so often, when nobody else would venture out on her, that later, when I started my water skiing, I felt no sense of danger, no fear, even without a life jacket."

Eventually Ralph let his father and brothers pursue their clamming and accepted a job, which promised a little more real cash money.

And the family needed every cent it could lay its hands on.

Naturally, Ralph's new job was a job on the Lake.

14. THE FISHERMAN

Ralph Samuelson, future wielder of water skies, became a fisherman—like St. Peter, a wielder of nets.

He was hired by another habitué of the Lake, gruff, but kindhearted Zack Nihart, heavy-set, 5 feet, 10 inches, quick, alert.

Ralph was only 11 years old, but behaved like a man.

On June 28 of that year, 1914, Archduke Francis Ferdinand and his wife, Sophia, heirs to the Austrian throne, were assassinated at Sarajevo, Bosnia.

Within days, Europe was doing what she always did with such deadly thoroughness—making war.

The event left little impression on the men and boys trying to make a living on peaceful Lake Pepin.

That trouble was all so very, very far away. If the damn fools in Europe wanted to kill each other that was their foolish business. Where the devil was Sarajevo anyway? Or Austria, for that matter?

Ralph had to learn new skills. He didn't mind as long as he could do it on or near his Lake.

That love affair was becoming so serious that at times Ralph would wander out all by himself, stand and stare at his Lake, marvel at her endless moods—ranging from violent, angry storms that slapped waves against the rocks like an ocean, to its sleepy moods when the water was a sheet of polished granite.

While the symbol of clamming had been the iron bar, adorned with its charm bracelet of dangling crow-foot iron hooks, the status symbol of the Lake Pepin fisherman was his net.

To young Ralph Samuelson that net became something to respect, fear at times.

It was over a mile long, attached to a rope even longer. The whole thing almost reached from the shore of Minnesota to the shore of Wisconsin at a narrower point of the Lake. It took a whole half a day to haul it in, loaded with enough fish to fill 200 sugar barrels—containers easily and cheaply acquired as discards in those days.

But before the net could be hauled in, it had to be cast out.

That was dangerous.

The whole mountain of mesh would be loaded each morning on a barge about 40 feet long and 10 feet wide, with sides four feet high. The barge was hauled by a soggy launch, with the romantic misnomer of "Blue Goose." It wasn't blue, actually scared the wild, white geese that occasionally decided to drop down on the Lake. But the name appealed to the old water rat, Nihart.

To unload the net the launch would make a large circle on the Lake, the net would flow out like a weird monster with a coarse-grained, lacy skin. And the person who had to throw out the cork line, marking the position of the net to which it was attached, had to be nimble, quick, daring. For as the barge moved on inexorably, the line running out with the net sometimes became tangled, and had to be unknotted fast. Woe unto the careless novice who got his hand or foot caught in that snarled-up strand. He simply went over the side with it. And trying to swim with your foot held by the coil of a slimy rope wasn't easy. Sometimes terminal.

"That rope tried to get me many times, but never quite made it. I was too quick," Ralph recalled years later. "But I do know a man who was drowned that way."

In the afternoon, the process was reversed, the net was hauled in by a big power winch. By now it was filled with a weird assortment of fish, including carp, catfish, bluegills, sturgeon, and game fish—bass, northern, pike, walleyes, crappies.

An effort was made to sort them out. The game fish were supposed to be tossed back, although some of the more palatable were kept for home consumption. The rest must be lugged off the boat in boxes, sometimes weighing 200 pounds each.

All the finny creatures were dumped into the barrels, with liberal chunks of ice, garnered from Lake Pepin the previous winter—and off they went by train to Chicago and New York.

The carp were especially welcome in New York. Ralph had never heard of Gefilte Fish, or Jewish New Year carp, but he packed them anyway.

It was work, but there were lighter moments.

Old Zack Nihart, often unshaven, with a stubby beard, his clothes always smelling of fish, took a liking to the absolutely fearless young water rat, Ralph.

It was Zack, so Ralph remembered, who gave him his nickname, "Sammy," which stuck ever since. Soon everybody was calling him "Sammy."

Ralph seemed to have an uncanny affinity with the Lake. Zack would make bets with him about the number of barrels each particular haul would deliver.

The boy would stare at the water, look at the sky, check wind and temperature, and make a bet with Zack.

It was weird. Time after time Ralph won. It became a by-word in town. "That 'Sammy' seems to have some sort of inside information about what's going on in that Lake. Zack lost another bet today."

Not that the bets made Ralph rich. The winner got a banana split, worth all of 10 cents.

Many a Saturday night Ralph and Zack would stroll over to Jane's Ice Cream Parlor on South Washington, and the lad would gorge himself on banana splits. One night he almost reached the point of no return. Four times that week he had won a bet on the number of barrels of fish.

He had to consume four splits. And those banana dishes were big—one whole, giant-size banana, three scoops of ice cream, vanilla, strawberry, chocolate, with rich chocolate fudge on top, mixed with marshmallows and raspberry juice, and two cherries on top of that. Cost, two nickels.

Ralph refused to bet the following week!

Zack had a habit of playing tricks on those he liked, especially "Sammy."

He had acquired a section of Central Point, north of the city, known as Rest Island. At one time historic Hotel Russel had been located there, and had drawn many tourists; it had fallen into disrepair. Rest Island later became Nihart's Nemesis, when he tried to raise silver foxes there—a venture that ended in bankruptcy. But, for the moment, Zack was using part of his property to raise melons.

While the net was being pulled in slowly by the men in charge of the power winch, Zack and some of his crew had time to relax. They sometimes did it by sitting on the shore, eating watermelons.

Zack, teasing his favorite assistant, would find some excuse to send "Sammy" to the opposite side of the point, ostensibly to pick up and bury the fish that had been mortally injured by the mile-long net and had been washed up on shore.

By the time "Sammy" had finished his chore, there was no watermelon left.

Ralph found a playful way to get even. Doing things with malice was never part of Ralph's philosophy of life. He wasn't brought up that way.

So the next time he was assigned to a dead fish burial detail, he shuffled off to the other side with his spade as always. But once out of sight, he dashed into Zack's patch, thumped several melons until he found one that sounded right, plucked it, ran to the beach. Letting the unfortunate fish rot in the sun, he sat down under a linden tree and ate the whole thing by himself.

For three days that worked fine. On the fourth, Zack sneaked up on his errant helper, caught him by the seat of his dungarees—as old Walt Anderson had done years ago—and tossed him bodily into the Lake, to the accompaniment of raucous laughter from the rest of the crew.

That made it two points for Zack and only one for "Sammy."

It was Ralph's turn.

The opportunity to even the score came a few days later.

The net had been hauled in; the barge was loaded to its non-existent plimsol line with fish, many of them still flopping.

Zack was on the bow of his "Blue Goose" while Ralph was standing on the barge alongside. He carried his long pike, a useful tool to subdue a net. With his pike extended, Ralph managed to reach Zack, busy giving directions for landing.

Ralph pushed.

Zack lost his balance, made an ungraceful, head-over-heels entry into the Lake.

He kept his head above water in spite of his boots and heavy trousers, spluttered, blew out water like an incensed whale, and found his voice.

Lake Pepin, which had heard curses of French voyageurs, tough American Fort Snelling soldiers, and weather-hardened fur pirates as they cordelled one of their loaded keelboats off a hidden sandbar with a line hitched to a tree, had never heard such malediction in any language.

Zack wasted no time trying to swim for shore. He made for the barge—and Ralph.

The boy saw purpose in those angry splashes of the fisherman's flailing arms. It was time to leave.

Ralph took a dive into the water, hoping for a getaway on shore. He reached land, started to run. Zack was close behind, and gaining, still bellowing curses. Ralph sprinted for the nearest maple tree, jumped, got hold of a limb, pulled himself up, started to climb.

It was a mistake.

Zack came up that tree like a cat after a wood duck. He caught up with his young pike bearer, and without ceremony, reverting to the cave man in him, bit Ralph in the rump—hard.

Not once, twice, three times.

"I had teeth marks on my behind for weeks," Ralph remembered, rubbing his left buttock as if the sores were still there. "The old coot had his mouth full of tobacco, in spite of the water he had gulped. It's a wonder I didn't get a case of gangrene."

The joke was on Ralph. The escapade was a conversation piece all the rest of the summer. Not that Ralph minded. He always enjoyed attention.

And now that they were even, Ralph thought it was time to get something off his chest.

The next Saturday, when Nihart was watching him eat his second banana split he had won that week, the boy broached the subject, between swallows.

"Zack—I been thinking," he began.

"Not good for kids to think. Let older folks do the thinking for you."

"No, really, Zack, I been thinking."

"How can you eat and think at the same time? Eat!"

"I can, too, eat and think. I been thinking—know any place where I could get a job with a little more money?"

"More money? What you want with money? You're getting all your banana splits free. Still don't know how the devil you do it."

"Zack, why don't you give me a raise?"

Zack Nihart's big, florid face was screwed up in pain, "What's that?"

"A raise. I think I should have a raise."

"There you go again, thinkin'. You? A raise? Hell, you ain't worth the money I pay you now. Now finish that banana split, if you want to go to the movie."

"No raise?"

"Hell, no. No raise."

But came next Saturday (he had won only one bet that week) Ralph found an extra $5 in his pay envelope. He tried to thank Zack at Jane's ice cream counter. Zack shut him up.

"I told you, you ain't worth the money I paid you. Now you ain't worth the extra money I'm payin' you. Hurry up. We're late."

That was Nihart's last summer before he went from fishing to fox raising, with unhappy consequences.

The consequences were unhappy for young Ralph, too. He was out of a job!

It may be a reflection on the young lad's daring, or perhaps his growing sense of responsibility, that he borrowed money from friends and bought himself his own secondhand launch, named "Gosoon," joining his older brother, Ben, his younger brother, Donald, and his father. Clamming had once again become a family affair. Charles, age 8, joined in the work after school, and on weekends.

Now, four clamming launches went out at dawn, sometimes floating downstream side by side, stopping at noon to let the boys eat their heavy sandwiches of ham, cheese, sausage, hard-boiled eggs, homemade strawberry sauce, or applesauce, packed in tin pails by mother Mary and sister Harriet. The boys would talk things over, make plans. Ralph loved to make plans; was always making plans.

And then, without warning, tragedy struck the family a blow … and Lake Pepin recorded a new tragedy.

15. THE BROTHERS

The Samuelson brothers loved to work together, play together, swim, fish, hunt together, not only on Lake Pepin, "which was indeed, a national and natural flyway for migrating ducks and geese." Sometimes they used the old family car, packed it full of every possible gear, including guns and fishing rods, drove north on the graveled roads, through a cluttered section of St. Paul, past the magnificent State Capitol, and eventually stopped at some small lake, of which Minnesota has an estimated 15,000.

There for a week they'd either camp by a reedy shore, where not too long before Chippewas had ambushed Sioux and Winnebagos while they were gathering wild rice; or they'd live in one of the small vacation cabins sprung up for the use of tourists.

On Sunday, August 17, 1914, with far-away Europe beginning to go up in the flames of World War I, the boys and their father decided to fish closer to home—on Lake Pepin.

The day was hot, windless, cloudy, a good day for walleyes.

The Samuelsons discovered there were too many for one boat, so they used a small craft equipped with an outboard motor, and a flat-bottomed skiff, which they towed north two miles to Central Point, not too far from the spot where Ralph used to eat Zack's watermelons.

"What happened we couldn't even blame on Lake Pepin," Ralph recalled "There were no big waves, no storm, just a few ripples."

Ben, a teen, and the youngest brother, Charlie, age 8, were in the skiff. Ralph, 11, Donald, 9, and their father were in the boat.

"The skiff had two seats in the center, one in the back, another in front," Ralph remembered. "Ben sat in front, Charlie in the rear. They threw out their lines and waited. We were a few yards away."

As often before, Ben had brought his shotgun along, for sometimes canvasbacks, teals or mallards, nesting in the marshes, flew over, and Ben brought back ducks when he didn't catch fish.

On this day he laid his shotgun across the two center seats, the safety catch on. The weapon was within reach; ducks didn't wait.

Ben thought he might get more mileage out of the skiff with a third bamboo fishing pole hanging out over the side. The butt end of that pole was pushed under the heavy gun, to hold it steady, as the boat rocked gently.

While the two boys were busy watching their own poles, and just as Charlie had a bite on his, it happened!

Through the motion of the boat, the end of the unmanned pole must have, somehow, released the gun's safety catch. Then, by some freak coincidence nobody was ever able to explain, it touched the trigger of the loaded gun. The barrel spit its load of buckshot straight at blond, lively little Charlie and hit his right leg above the knee, almost tearing it off.

What followed was never clear in Ralph's blurred mind.

Charles screamed; Ben yelled for assistance. Everybody tried to apply a tourniquet. Ralph connected the skiff to the very slow outboard, and frantically they chugged for Lake City and a doctor.

They got there too late; Charlie had lost so much blood. He looked dead before he could be carried into the house. He died two hours later.

The Samuelsons had lost one boy, little Clarence, age 2, but that was before Ralph was born. This was different.

The melancholy family funeral brought them closer together than ever. They laid young Charles next to his brother Clarence on the family plot in the Lakewood Cemetery, with its rows upon rows of arbor vitae evergreens, planted there by the same Eric Wilson for whom Ralph had worked at the Jewell Nursery.

Tragedy or not, in spite of the empty place at the table, the empty bed upstairs in the big bedroom, heated in winter only by the pipe from the stove below, life had to go on.

Life did.

For several summers the Samuelsons dedicated their time to clamming, in all kids of weather—windy, stormy, foggy, humid, or fair; the winters, to working on the boats, barges, equipment; while Mary's shuttle flitted like a hummingbird between the two sets of warp thread of whatever carpet she was weaving at the time.

And eventually World War I reached even the dreamy shore of Lake Pepin. It nabbed Ben.

The farewells at the brown-painted Chicago, Milwaukee, St. Paul railroad station, beautifully landscaped by the same Eric Wilson, were traumatic.

After that, occasional letters from Ben kept the family informed—even after he left New York on a troop ship, landed in France, got into the trenches, experienced Chateau Thierry, and the Meuse Argonne.

Ben wrote about the French people who lived on small farms, plowed with horses in tandem, lived from hand to mouth; and about the cooties, the muck, the rain, the killing, the homesickness.

He stayed a private, but was promoted to letter-carrier, riding a motorcycle with sidecar to and from the front. And when the "War to End All Wars" finally itself ended, at the eleventh hour of the eleventh day of the eleventh month of 1918, he had survived.

Ben came home a hero. Today, a military plaque marks his grave on the same Lake City cemetery plot where lie his parents, his brothers, and his wife.

Nobody was happier to see Ben than his brother Ralph. For it was Ben, with his boat, driven by the same old Saxon motor, who eventually helped him do what he had been dreaming of doing—gliding along the surface of Lake Pepin on skis.

While Ben was away, Ralph had not wasted any time. He had perfected his stunts on his aquaplane, sometimes riding double with friend Red Walstrom.

Red—Maurice—another good-natured Swede, after he retired to his neat, well-furnished home on North Lakeshore Drive in Lake City, grinned when he recalled the escapades on that surfboard, as he called Ralph's aquaplane.

"We were crazy—fearless," said the former construction engineer, a tinge of red still visible in his graying hair. "And that Ralph Samuelson. Sure, we all thought he was nuts. But we also knew that nobody could drown us. We just had that feeling. Partly defiance. Everybody was still scared of our Lake—that "Sea Wing" disaster hung over us. But, with Ralph around, you began to trust Lake Pepin again.

"So we did stunts together. He'd stand on my shoulders, and he wasn't too light, while I balanced on that crazy, bouncing board. Or he'd stand on his head. Sometimes he'd ride on an old backless chair set on the board, even stand on his head on the chair.

"I guess one reason Ralph was interested in me was natural enough. I was working at the time, earning money, while Ralph didn't have much cash. So I sometimes helped him out when it came to buying things he needed, like a rope, or gasoline for his brother's launch. It was a great time, especially when we put on those water carnivals in the 1920s.

"Yes, I guess I did have something to do with bringing Ralph to the point where he actually skied on water. He got the honor. That's all right with me.

"Anyway, neither of us ever made any money off those water stunts, not even after people began to hear about us and came to watch; even paid some sort of admission to get past the snow fence we used as a barrier. All the money went to the city, never to us. We were glad to do it for our hometown. I wonder if kids would do as much today? I guess maybe some would," Red Walstrom snickered, sitting there on the back porch of his home. "One thing came out of this. 'Sammy' is now giving God all the glory and honor for his invention. I suppose that's good. He sure wasn't thinking much about God in them days, though."

Ralph admits it freely; Red was right. God meant absolutely nothing in those days. But every year, his love affair with Lake Pepin grew.

"Many a time did I get tumbled around by that old Lake, sometimes in storms that kept even my brothers and my father home," Ralph said. "Of course, in her softer moments, when she just lay there and dozed like a beautiful young girl sunning herself, were wonderful, too."

A special day always came for the whole town when the ice finally went out of Lake Pepin in the spring.

To Ralph Samuelson, that day meant he could soon be on and in water again, instead of skating on top of ice or scooting along on his iceboat.

Often, bets were made about the day and hour when the cold stuff would finally give up.

Ice was important to Lake City, with its two ice storing plants. Ole Beckman's, and W.E. Sprague's.

As soon as the ice was over 12 inches thick—preferably when it was 24 to 30 inches—it was cut into blocks, 24 inches wide and 48 inches long, first with a one-horse ice cutter and, after 1919, with gasoline motors and saws.

The blocks were hauled up long inclines into the ice sheds packed in layers of sawdust for insulation, and delivered during the summer to stores, and homes that had iceboxes. The ice was used indiscriminately to cool drinks, without danger of pollution apparently, to pack the carp for New York and Chicago—and to preserve corpses in pre-embalming days.

Some of Lake Pepin's ice was loaded into freight cars in be-low-zero weather and shipped to Chicago.

Lake Pepin threw off her icy mantle on many different dates in spring and never in the same way.

Sometimes the cover would just get mushy and silently float away, tired and defeated by sun and warm rains; more often, after booming and crackling all winter, the solid surface would smash itself into floes that buckled and crashed and crunched them-selves into formidable mountains along the shore.

And every year, the more adventurous packets competed with each other to get through that Lake first. Lake Pepin was always the very last barrier to open up between St. Louis and St. Paul. The ship that got to the Twin Cities first won an all-season free berth as a prize, and could tie a broom to its smokestack to prove it.

At times, captains dared to go through prematurely. More than one vessel was literally shoved on the rocks by Lake Pepin ice or even sheered in half by tons of those floes.

During these dramatic breakups—sometimes in March, more frequently during the first two weeks in April when persistent north winds would drive what seemed like millions of tons of angry, resisting ice southward, there to disappear for another year—Ralph would stand on the shore and be almost overawed by Nature's grandeur.

But once the ice was out, it wouldn't take more than a week or 10 days before the Samuelson clan had its clamming rigs out, eager to discover how good was this year's crop.

Meanwhile, each year, Ralph Samuelson came closer to the

day—July 2, 1922—when Red Walstrom's bobbing surfboard was dramatically displaced by two long, broad, gliding water skis, and Lake Pepin flowed into history again.

{3}
Section

16. THE EXHIBITIONIST

After his first successful attempt at water skiing, Ralph Samuelson displayed characteristics some of his friends and relatives had encountered before: tenacity, singleness of purpose, determination to stick it out, ability to take knocks, unwillingness to get discouraged or plain stubbornness.

Every minute he could spare from clamming, he practiced skiing until he had really mastered the big boards. He could cross the wake of Ben's launch—and it was a big, awkward wake—swing out as far as a new, longer rope would let him, deliberately cut back and forth at fantastic angles to develop more speed.

One of his original skis cracked when he tried to leap over an especially large wave.

He made a duplicate pair. Those two skis have survived, and are on display at the Minnesota Historical Society Museum in St. Paul. That was the pair that finally lifted Samuelson out of his anonymity—but not until they were 41 years old!

Ralph made a few improvements on his new boards—reinforced the bent tips with thin, narrow strips of metal, made especially for him at Pearson's blacksmith shop. He padded the center of each ski with rubber matting; set his leather straps farther back to make it easier to manipulate the unwieldy things; labeled them R and L; painted his initials RWS on each. Aside from that, they were identical with the first pair—eight feet long, nine inches wide.

Fred Rose, the clammer, had meanwhile purchased a launch called "Pepin," from one of the town's rich residents, who owned a summer mansion south of town, a place that was to play a role in Ralph's life later.

"Pepin" could churn along at about 25 miles per hour, which made skiing a little more exciting—and easier.

Fred agreed to pull Ralph if the city would pay for the gas. The city did—75 cents for an entire Sunday afternoon's hauling.

Ralph's audience was growing. A natural showman, he combined aquaplaning and water skiing on the same program. He and Red Walstrom would do their stunts with the aquaplane, real daredevil stuff. As top billing, Ralph skied.

Then he had a bit of luck.

The sports editor of the *St. Paul Daily News* heard about this crazy business going on at Lake City, 60 miles south, drove down, incognito, was impressed, talked to Ralph, suggested he do something bigger than just showing off before the home folks.

Probably because he was in need of pictures for his sports section and didn't want to lug his equipment too far, or because he had friends at White Bear, a resort area nearer St. Paul, the editor had Ralph do his act before the Kiwanis Club at the White Bear Yacht Club.

Fee? No fee, of course—only a free meal. But Ralph rose to the occasion in a grand manner, skied his heart out, and his feet sore behind William Peet's motorboat. And the following Sunday Ralph Samuelson's picture leaped at the readers not only from the *Daily News*, but the venerable *St. Paul Pioneer Press.*

After that brief but significant brush with publicity, Ralph became even more daring in his performances—so much so, that some of his neighbors began to call him a show-off, a ham.

To be considered a ham in your hometown is not pleasant. In a community of much less than 3,000 at the time, where gossip spread fast, and as in most small towns where everybody knew at least a little about everybody else's business, Ralph was no longer a crackpot, and "a little off upstairs," but "that young Samuelson squirt who thinks he's somebody special."

He was something special, but he took the criticism in stride.

Eventually, the word got around to the neighboring farms and the other small towns, even to the burgeoning Mayo Clinic city of Rochester 30 miles away that on Lake Pepin a guy was actually skiing on top of the water on boards he called water skis.

Who first got the idea, whether the Lake City Commercial Club, or the Lyons Club, forerunners of the present Chamber of Commerce, city officials, or just some promotion-minded individual seems not known today. But, eventually, Ralph Samuelson became the star performer at regular weekly water carnivals, while spectators sat on rough benches, on the grass, or the gravelly beach, listened to homemade band music, and watched that crazy Samuelson do his stunts.

The next spring Ralph got his skis out almost as soon as the water was free of ice.

The city fathers decided to build a small bandstand by the shore, facing the cove where Ralph was performing, an area now known as Ohuta Park.

Bigger and bigger Sunday afternoon crowds of more or less fascinated spectators gathered—to chat, eat picnic lunches, and munch peanuts and popcorn dispensed by Zump Adolph, first from a horse-drawn popcorn wagon, then later from a motor-driven van, and hear Sousa marches and popular songs like "Listen to the Mockingbird."

The small entrance fee collected at the snow-fence gate, as Red Walstrom indicated, didn't go to the performers. The money was eventually used to make a deposit on the purchase by the city of the very land the fence was on, later to become Lake City's marina.

17. THE GIRL

Ralph was a self-styled lady's man, even in his early 20s, the cause of some jealousy among contemporary swains.

Some of them hinted, 50 years later, that when they went sparking girls in Red Wing or Wabasha, not to mention the Lake City girls, and Ralph was along, he was often a nuisance.

With his boyish face masked in complete, sweet innocence, he'd secretly tip off some of the young ladies about what their ardent beaux were really saying about them in private. Usually it worked to Ralph's advantage, according to these jealous rivals.

But then he himself fell into one of love's traps, baited with a little blond Norwegian beauty.

Helen Anderson lived just a few blocks from Ralph's busy menage. He had never paid much attention to her. But then, one summer, suddenly there she was "all peaches and cream," a favorite description of perfect beauty in the 1920s.

Ralph became helplessly ensnared in the summer of 1924, when Lake City officials decided it was time to bring their beautiful Lake more enticingly to the attention of more tourists—too many of whom went barreling through town in their Hupmobiles, Dorts, Darts, Whippets, Willys Knights, Studebakers, Essexes, Chevrolets, Dodges, and Packards, raising clouds of yellow dust, without ever realizing that Lake City had bathing facilities, Sunday band concerts, and spectacular water ski exhibitions performed by a local celebrity.

The answer was a genuine water pageant—with a parade and lighted boats at night, "a glorious spectacle," as it was billed.

The theme of the event would be Maiden Rock.

Legendary Maiden Rock was a precipitous bluff on the Wisconsin side of the river, 400 feet high, which Ralph and his brothers had climbed often—as had thousands of tourists in the early days of luxury riverboat excursions.

Even Mark Twain relates how, when he passed through Lake Pepin, he was regaled with the story of the famous brink from which a beautiful Sioux maiden, Winona, was supposed to have hurled herself in despair when prevented from marrying the young Chippewa she loved.

There were skeptics, including Ralph, who pointed out that the area had as many versions of the legend as there were tellers. Some claimed Winona was the daughter of Chief Red Wing; others insisted her father was the circumspect, abstemious, teetotaler Wabasha, who had his village down at what is now Winona.

Ralph knew Winona simply meant "first-born," that every chief had his Winona, and that Indian women had a great deal of freedom of choice about their mates.

But whether the legend lacked substance or not, people loved to hear about it, read about it, and especially see it acted out—this time with an artificial bluff made of papier-mâché, cloth, canvas, scaffolds, and ladders, from which a comely female took a dive into Lake Pepin, with spotlights on her short, deerskin skirt.

None of which would have affected Ralph Samuelson's healthily budding libido too much, had not Helen been chosen to be queen of the pageant parade.

So there she was—all glittered up for the occasion, with a crown of simulated diamonds and pearls on her golden hair, costume jewelry all over her shimmering white gown, her well-shaped bosom high and proud, riding on the flat bottom of an old truck labeled "Queen of the Water Carnival." Floats in front of her and behind her were dwarfed by her beauty—or so it seemed to Ralph to whom she looked positively ravishing.

That evening, his emotions were seething as she let him kiss her not once—but twice—right on the lips.

But apparently Helen's parents didn't think there was much of a future for a young nut who spent all his spare time fussing around on those crazy skis on that dangerous Lake. They warned Helen against this foolish daredevil, who would definitely be drowned any day now.

During Helen and Ralph's love affair, she undoubtedly inspired Ralph Samuelson to do something even more dramatic.

It was probably his desire to make an impression on the lovely Helen, to show his bravery and prowess, which encouraged him the next summer, 1925, to create another first.

Ralph Samuelson became the first human being to make a water ski jump!

18. THE JUMPER

Attendants at any one of thousands of water ski shows given annually all over the world can see men and women, boys and girls, make fantastic jumps on skis. It is one of the standard events at every water ski tournament or carnival.

Said Ralph Samuelson, the first jumper on skis, "I continued water skiing and putting on water shows at Lake City, but never did anything sensational until 1925 when I got the idea for a water ski jump. I believe this inspiration came because I wanted to do something more bold, more daring, enlarge my capabilities"—and incidentally display his manliness before the lovely Helen?

It may also have been a natural outgrowth of boyish activities. Thousands of times Ralph and his friends had jumped off everything available on the Lake—floating trees, boats, and especially the old diving platform of rough, water-soaked, weather-beaten planks chained to barrels—probably vinegar or beer barrels, of which the town had plenty.

Each fall, that diving dock was carefully hauled on shore so the battering rams of Lake Pepin's ice floes wouldn't grind it to kindling.

Ralph got permission from whatever councilman was in charge of the waterfront, a job ably filled for years to come by that same "punk who was there when it all began," as he called himself in later interviews, harbor master Ben Simons, to move that dock out into deeper water and remove two of the floating supports.

Consequently, the platform was submerged about 12 inches below water at one end, and projected above the Lake some five feet on the other, forming a 30 degree incline.

The contraption, Ralph recalled was only about four feet wide, and 16 feet long.

Again he had to learn the hard way, through trial and error and effort.

Ralph convinced his skeptical brother that he could leave the water, slide up that incline on his skis, and jump back into the Lake, without letting go of the rope, if Ben would steer the boat close enough so he could swing out and get the skis on the planks.

They practiced for several hours, Ralph daring to maneuver himself closer and closer to the raft.

Finally he did it! He got his skis on the submerged end of the dock, was pulled upward to the very top—and stuck there!

The rope was jerked out of his hands, and Ralph tumbled off, head first, without his skis. Luckily, he had learned to get his feet out of those leather straps under any and all emergency conditions.

"Pioneering has its thrills, as you are never quite sure what you can do until you prove it to yourself," Ralph commented on that incident decades later.

One thing was obvious to him at once: The surface of that

dry, rough old platform had to be greased.

His father had lost his grocery store, so Ralph hiked to Ludwig's on Center Street, the man who had taken over his father's location, and bought or borrowed several pounds of lard that had gone rancid.

On shore, idlers shook their heads in amazement. That Ralph Samuelson had really gone crazy? He was smearing lard all over the diving platform!

Twice Ralph lost his footing on that ramp, while coating it, so greasy it was. He didn't mind.

He hoped this time his stunt would work. At least, if he got splinters in his rump now, they'd be well lubricated.

Again Brother Ben taxied his smoking boat close enough so Ralph could get his skis over the submerged end of the platform, stinking of rotting pork.

This time, Ralph went up like a greased pig and over the rim like a flying squirrel, or a flying fish.

Nobody was there to measure the length of that first historic jump; but before the day was over, Ralph could jump 50 to 60 feet, depending on Ben's speed.

Ralph admitted it took some time to learn how to keep his knees from buckling when he came down with those heavy boards, which landed on the surface of Lake Pepin as if they were made of concrete.

But thus, on July 8, 1925, three years and six days after he had become the first human being to ski on water, Ralph W. Samuelson became the first to do a water ski jump.

"And I never knew what I had started," Ralph later commented.

19. THE SPEED KING

Something even more dramatic happened a month later. Ralph became the original speed skier—first towed by a boat equipped with a weird, discarded airplane motor; then behind a World War I Curtiss Flying Boat, powered by a Spanish 220 horsepower engine using a pusher propeller.

Owner of the Curtiss was Captain Walter Bullock.

Robert W. Fick, prominent businessman at Lake City, summarized his memories for me about how Ralph came to be a speed skier, and added another word to the ski vocabulary.

> ...A small urchin of seven, [I] was one of the several hundred skeptics lining the shores of the Lake when Samuelson achieved what everybody then thought impossible—and insanely dangerous: first skiing behind a boat powered with a Wright Whirlwind aeroplane engine, mounted on a 10-foot high steel tripod, at 60 miles an hour; and later at 80 miles per hour, towed behind a Curtiss MF Flying Boat of World War I vintage.
>
> Maurice Walstrom, still a Lake City resident, owned the boat, which sounded like an airplane in flight, in fact, it could be heard 10 miles away, but which periodically submerged, because the bow nosed down with the thrust of the airplane propeller 10 feet in the air, instead of in the water, underneath the boat. ... In 1925, Walter Bullock, an early Northwest Airlines pilot ... came to Lake City with his flying boat, grandfather of the later pontoon planes.

It was this craft that pulled Ralph Samuelson and made him the first real speed skier—on water.

Walter Bullock's name was later inscribed in the OX-5 Club of America, the Aviation Hall of Fame, Hammondsport, New York.

After retiring, Walter spent much of his time reconstructing old World War I planes, at his place in Lakeville, a community of 7,500, south of the Twin Cities.

In a conversation, he recalled what happened that week of August 20, 1925, on Lake Pepin.

"At the time the whole thing was just another incident to me.

I flew directly to Lake Pepin, a lake large enough to land on in any weather, simply to give people a ride, and make an honest buck. Fee was $2 a ride.

"Along came this tall, young chap, and asked if I'd give him a different kind of ride, by pulling him behind my flying boat. He argued it would attract enough attention so I'd get more regular riders. He was pretty persuasive and sold me.

"I had no idea at the time that I was participating in anything remotely historic when I told him, 'Sure. Why not?'

"Well, we did it several times, successfully.

"I have no regrets. I only wish I knew what became of that old Curtiss Flying Boat. I'd certainly reconstruct it. It would be a fine addition to my collection, and an unusual addition to water ski souvenirs."

Samuelson was more graphic in his recollection of what happened.

"I had never found a boat fast enough to satisfy me," he remembered. "Not even Red Walstrom's noisy 10-foot-high contraption.

"But that day when I saw Walter come down out of the sky in his flying boat, and later take up some passengers, I wondered if a man couldn't ride behind this flying machine, if it wouldn't go too high in the air.

"As always, I was going on the assumption that you never know what you can do, until you try it.

"Those were the days when life preservers were not available, at least not the kind you could ski with, like the special ski jackets of today. So I always performed without them.

"When I approached Walter with my request, he admitted he had never seen a pair of water skis before; and wasn't at all sure that I could even ride on them behind a boat, to say nothing of doing it behind a plane.

"I persuaded him it would do no harm to try. At the worst, I'd simply fall off.

"This took place on Tuesday, August 18. Walter told me to get a long rope; I sure did. Instead of the usual 100 feet of clothesline, I got one 200 feet long. The day was quiet and hot, the water had hardly a ripple on it. I guess old Lake Pepin was holding her breath, or something.

"The plane was moored near the end of Lake City Point, the triangle where the marina and the trailers are. People were looking the plane over, and consequently quite a number saw me make my first attempt at riding behind a plane.

"I tied my line to a lower strut, and Walter taxied out into the Lake. When I reached the end of my rope, I was ready, and waved my hand for him to go—and he did.

"At first I thought the pusher prop would blow me right over, the wind was that strong. The propeller also picked up water which hit me like bullets, right in the face.

"When the plane reached speed enough for a take-off, Walter pulled back the stick, and the plane tried to lift. But since there wasn't any wind, it bounced right back, hit the water, and then took off—a little too high.

"That yanked me clear off my feet! I actually became airborne for a few seconds. During the process, I lost my skis, of course, and eventually landed on my stomach. I let go the rope, hoping that would stop my undesired, unorthodox skiing. But I was going so fast, I skidded on my belly for nearly a city block.

"My first thought was not for my safety, but whether I had lost my swimming suit. It was still hanging on me, although a bit torn. And all I got out of the escapade was some slightly burned skin.

"Walter decided to wait for more breeze for a better take-off. We were lucky. The next day, Wednesday, August 19, we had our typical summer northwest wind. This time, Walter made a smooth take-off and managed to keep the plane low.

"We started at the same spot, and before I knew what was happening, I was skimming along so fast that in what seemed seconds we were scooting past Central Point, three miles above Lake City.

"Walter slowed enough to make a turn on the water, and then speeded up again toward town. I thought my arms would be pulled right out of my sockets. But I managed to hang on until we got back to Lake City, where Walter set his machine down for a landing.

"He told me we had gone 60 miles an hour. I had never gone more than 25.

"But that was only the beginning. Walter and I were both born promoters, I guess, at least I felt like one. So we had handbills printed at the *Wabasha County Leader* shop on West Central. Then we actually flew over Red Wing, 17 miles north, and as far as Rochester, 30 miles south, and to Wabasha and other towns, letting those colored poop sheets flutter down like pigeons with broken wings."

The text announced in no uncertain phrases the great event about to take place on Lake Pepin the following Sunday, August 25, when a "death-defying ride on water skis would be performed behind a gravity-defying flying boat."

"We were taking a chance," admitted Ralph. "If the weather had been bad, we would have been stymied. Luck was with us. Sunday was fair, warm, but with a southwest wind instead a northwester. And people! Our promotion paid off, handsomely. They had come by the thousands—by car, horse and buggy, bicycle, on foot. They lined the shore, standing and sitting three-deep.

"We couldn't take off toward Central Point because of this southwest wind, so we loaded the water skis and the rope in the plane and flew to Central Point and set her down.

"After tying the rope to the plane again, I gave Walter the go-ahead sign, and he really did take off. The plane was airborne in seconds, with the favorable wind. He held her low, and I managed to hang on to that old iron ring, although I was sure I'd be minus an arm any second.

"That was the fastest ride on water I ever had in my life. In fact, it took many years before the record was broken—not by me, but somebody in Florida, I think. I had water skied at 80 miles an hour!

"Walter flew right between the old diving tower at the spot where the diving platform used to stand, and the shore lined with people. I could hear them screech with astonishment—and fright—as I went by less than 400 feet from them.

"I probably would never have had a record of this historic event, which could, of course, have cost me my life, had not one of the Lake City gals, Grace Eaton, caught us with her old box Kodak. In fact, Grace took pictures of many of my attempts and always gave me one, bless her.

"It was sheer coincidence, of course, but Grace managed to get one picture of that flying boat and me just as Walter passed the diving tower. Kids had crawled up on that to get a better view. On the picture it looks as if they are standing right on the wing of the plane, which was hiding the tower. An unexpected little fringe benefit.

"I was tired after that event, but happy. Once more I had done something daring, something new!

"The next edition of the *Wabasha County Leader*, dated Friday, August 28, gave us a good write-up."

The *Leader* used a boxed headline: "Two Thousand People See Ralph Samuelson Perform Behind Seaplane."

The article in the favored upper right-hand corner of the front page, carried two photos, one of Ralph, built like a young Samson, with legs like palms, holding his two giant boards; the other a speed shot of Ralph behind the plane, wearing black trunks and a white shirt, clinging to his metal ring, his skis tilted so high only the last 12 inches were still in the water.

Said the un-bylined piece, in two monstrously long, old-fashioned paragraphs, not giving Ralph credit for being the first to do what he did, but bestowing honor enough on him:

> Last Sunday afternoon at the Lake City bathing beach 2,000 people were given a real thriller when Ralph Samuelson of this city did water skiing behind a seaplane that sped through the water at a dizzy pace and at times flew a few feet above the water. Ralph Samuelson again demonstrated his right to be termed 'the best water ski rider in the Northwest', by his performance Sunday afternoon. People from Rochester, Red Wing, Wabasha, and many other cities were in attendance to witness the water sports program of which the water skiing was the outstanding feature.
>
> Water sports programs such as the one last Sunday have done much to make the Lake City bathing beach one of the most popular recreation centers in southern Minnesota. Indications are that the attendance at the Lake City bathing beach next summer will far exceed that of this year.

The *Leader* thus indicated what time of year it was. In another few days, it would be Labor Day—and very few people ventured out on the water, or visited the beach after Labor Day. The season would be dead. Ralph had just made it under the wire.

It was to be his last performance for 1925. But it had been a great year, what with the water jump and the speed record.

"Walter Bullock, too, benefited from this event, and came back the next year, and we put on another good show," Ralph recalled. "But I never equaled the 80 miles an hour again.

"Perhaps it was just as good. I had had my thrill. I was satisfied—for a little while, at least.

"I was never satisfied with myself very long, of course. When the next adventure beckoned, I was ready.

"I sometimes wonder if our modern youngsters haven't lost some of that spirit of adventure. Perhaps that's because there aren't many new worlds left to conquer, unless they go out into space. ..."

{4}
Section

20. FLORIDA

Ralph's father, Charles, still had his spirit of adventure, in spite of his personal and business problems.

Whatever the reason, like so many others who wanted to get rich quick in the 1920s, he invested in Florida land, when that was considered the clever thing to do.

People talked in terms of millions, spent their life savings to get in on the boom.

Most of these boomers lost their bank accounts, their shirts, and some their sanity, when the Florida balloon burst, leaving only a few clever promoters rich enough to spend the rest of their dishonest days at Miami beaches, while the suckers crept back to snowy Minnesota and a dozen other states.

Charles's wasn't a big investment—only 10 acres, three miles from the coast; and one lot in a town to be called Lantana, 15 miles south of Palm Beach. Lantana, a community of over 7,000 in the 1970s, was just a speck on a speculator's map.

While Charles was convinced he'd soon be rich, conservative Mary, having lived with her husband for a few trying decades, had her doubts.

But Charles insisted on going south to inspect his acres.

He took Ralph, the most adventurous of his boys, to do the driving. Charles had never learned how.

They went in Ralph's six cylinder Essex, a black, two-door hardtop sedan.

The family farewells were tearful. It was like sending men off to Mars. Few people in Lake City had ever ventured, or cared to venture, on such a wild trip—2,250 miles of practically un-charted, partly unpaved roads? Unthinkable.

Would they ever see each other again?

Besides, it was in the middle of winter, right after Christmas, with the highways covered with snow. But at least the roads were frozen dry, and the pellets of solid gravel, chunks of ice, and loose snow clattered noisily, but harmlessly, against the big fenders and the wide running boards.

Ralph cranked his car, jumped in, shouted hasty farewells to hide the emotions he felt, and pointed the radiator south.

Down crooked old Route 61 they labored, around innumerable bluffs, to Winona, crossed the wide Mississippi on a bridge considered one of the wonders of the valley. Once on the Wisconsin side, they made it south to La Crosse, then inland to Madison, stopping at the Wisconsin Dells and by the side of the road to rest or eat whenever they were tired or hungry.

They avoided downtown Chicago, but couldn't escape its sprawling suburbs. The snow hadn't been handled properly by the few available snowplows and had instead been packed tight by trucks and cars. Ralph maneuvered his car on top of this hard-packed snow, sometimes two feet thick. The crust was solid enough, but like a gigantic washboard, over which they bumped and skidded for weary miles. The detour around Chicago seemed endless.

Later, on Route 39, out of Joliet, Illinois, they were caught behind a snowplow that laboriously scraped a single lane through new snow. It took two hours to cover five miles.

Once out of the snow zone, they made better time, but most days they couldn't conquer more than 100 miles.

The first real trouble pounced on them in Indiana.

Following some crude maps put out by gasoline companies, they found Highway 43. Most roads were designated by colors or combinations of colors painted on telephone or fence posts, or they were marked by numbers and flimsy signs put up by local merchants who tried to attract business, sometimes intentionally misrouting tourists into town on long, unnecessary detours.

To make up for lost time, Ralph was driving late. He crossed the historic old National Trail, now U.S. 40, running from Baltimore to San Francisco, marked then by stripes of red, white, and blue paint on every 10th telephone or telegraph pole, and reached Cloverdale, Indiana, a little town about 20 miles south of Greencastle, home of DePauw University.

It had been warmer that day, snow had melted, leaving the road a bottomless slough of freezing mud. And it was dark. The lights on the small car helped only a little. They hit some terrible mud holes—and suddenly the Essex stopped with a jolt. The whole front end sagged crookedly into the mud.

The right front wheel had come off. While the car had stopped, that wheel hadn't. It kept rolling in the dark, into a flat Indiana cornfield of reddish-yellow clay.

Before he recovered it, Ralph was muddier than the wheel.

But he finally found, it, after wading ankle deep, sometimes crawling on his knees, in slush and goo.

The tire was still intact, the spokes were okay. But by the glimmer of his flashlight, Ralph discovered he had ground out a wheel bearing.

"For a moment it looked as if our glorious trip, begun with

such bravado, was ending in the mud of Indiana," Ralph summed it up. "But soon my Swedish stubbornness came to my rescue. I'd be danged if I'd let one miserable little flattened wheel bearing defeat me!"

Ralph tramped through the muck back to Cloverdale, found a little garage by the side of the road still open. The sleepy owner came out with his wrecker, and pulled them back to town.

After what seemed an endless search through his cluttered inventory, the mechanic concluded he didn't have the proper bearing for an Essex wheel. Ford maybe, even Hupmobile, but Essex? Too high-class for him.

Ralph and his father spent a miserable night in a small hotel. The next day, the garage man drove them back to Greencastle. Sure enough, they found a bearing, put it into the wheel, paid their bill, a whopping $50, which made such an abysmal dent in their financial reserve that they hardly ate for days. But at least they were on their way again.

It was still cold, drizzly now, and sleety, until they got into Kentucky, always feeling their way, losing it, finding it again.

Slowly but inevitably they reached Nashville, Chattanooga, Atlanta, Jacksonville—each amazing in its own way—and finally Lantana by the sea.

During the latter part of the trip they slept in their tent to save hotel bills. One night, beside a gurgling mountain stream in the hills of Tennessee, their alfresco slumbers were disturbed by sudden, weird, ungodly sounds, such as Ralph had never heard. He tried to guess: Mountain lion? A strange nocturnal bird? Ghosts?

The solution was as simple as it was bizarre. As the noise came nearer, they hid behind a big log, until the apparition could be identified: a young mountain lad riding a mule, yodeling at the top of his voice. Ralph never found out, was a boy yodeling out of sheer exuberance or to give himself courage in the dark? Or was he a moonshiner, with a snort of his own joy juice too many?

Moonshiners they saw aplenty. Once, when they had lost their way, they stumbled on a still. They left in a hurry, after assuring a skeptical operator that they definitely were not revenuers.

Those were the days when counties, at times even individuals through whose land the highway meandered, looked upon the road as their private source of income and collected by means of toll gates or chained bridges.

One such, with a heavy chain across it, Ralph encountered on another dark night, after the toll collector had gone to bed. They had to wake him, and fork over 50 cents, plus 10 cents more for coming so late, before the Essex was allowed to cross a very narrow mountain stream on a very narrow mountain bridge.

Most of the time, they crossed streams by doing what came naturally, driving through them with water up to the oil pan.

They made Florida in about 10 days—Ralph had lost track.

What followed was not too happy a time in Ralph's life. For one thing, he never once got to use the skis he had so lovingly hauled down to Florida, strapped to the top of his car. He and his father had to spend their whole time building a little house to live in.

All around them, buildings were going up as if it were a Mississippi River paper town of the early 19th Century, when speculators, through gross and heartless misrepresentation, coaxed innocent, unsuspecting buyers to come thousands of miles to invest money in a town that looked beautifully complete and organized on phony maps, but didn't exist at all.

Many of the buildings in Lantana—houses, sheds, schools, barns, stores—were never finished. Eventually, they stood there like gray skeletons, reminding people for years of the foolishness of suckers and the cupidity of a few successful and clever speculators and con men.

Ralph confessed later that the 10 acres which he helped to clear all winter, on which he slaved willingly since Florida was an escape from the rugged Minnesota winter, could have been sold by his father for $10,000 at one point when the boom was still booming.

Somebody offered Charles Samuelson that in cash. Cash! Charles didn't take it. Like so many others, he was holding out for more. In a few years, the whole thing went back to waiting officials for taxes. Came spring, and Charles and Ralph motored patiently back to Minnesota.

One winter of such uncertainty was enough for Charles. He never went back to Florida to inspect investments, which had blown up in his face.

Ralph did go back—but for very different reasons.

21. DETROIT

Samuelson and Fate were marching along, side by side. But, as yet, the Father of Water Skiing had not been acknowledged as such by anybody.

Why?

Because nobody cared any more about who had "done it first on water skis" in 1926 than in 1922.

Whatever the reason, Ralph, now 23, decided he must branch out, leave home, make his way, earn his fortune, leave the nest, spread his wings, get-a-gittin', as some of his friends put it—or whatever other bromide might fit.

Ralph had a cousin in Detroit with whom he occasionally corresponded. The young fellow was working in the huge Ford complex. More than 10 years before, Henry Ford had raised basic wages from $2.40 for a 9-hour day, to $5 for an 8-hour day, thereby shocking industry around the world. His Dearborn plant had become the fabled Mecca for countless hopeful young men.

Ralph went to Detroit by train, actually got a job at the Ford plant, and worked there all winter.

Winters in Detroit are no worse than winters in Minnesota. But came spring, Ralph missed something.

Water. His Lake.

The idea of being cooped up inside a noisy factory while outside Nature was silently, mysteriously, recycling herself gave him heartburn.

Going back to Lake Pepin, however, seemed inadvisable—a certain admission of defeat, something Ralph didn't cherish.

But what if he could find himself a job more to his liking, outdoors, right there in Detroit?

"God was pulling the strings, I suppose," said Ralph. "He was guiding me in the direction He wanted me to go. Inadvertently, I went, not knowing why, or how. But I went—to a speedboat delivery, a small concern that rented out speedboats, and was located almost under the famous Detroit Belle Isle Bridge."

Ralph thought it a queer place to have a boat dock, a shed, an office. But there it was, renting out sleek Dodge Water Cars with OX-5 aviation engines, capable of forcing the hulls of sleek, glowing mahogany through the water at 35 miles an hour.

The boats were rented out to joy riders, wives of executives playing golf at the fancy Belle Isle Golf Course, society dames taking their visiting country friends out for a ride up and down the Detroit River, lovers, honeymooners, tourists—and bootleggers, although they were off the record.

To Ralph, these boats meant only one thing—vehicles to pull him over the water on his much-neglected skis!

He soon formed a special friendship with one of the pilots, Chester Stuart. He was a little short guy, according to Ralph, trying to make himself taller by wearing elevator shoes. But he liked Ralph.

The leasing company needed publicity. When Ralph came along with a new-fangled idea—skiing on gigantic boards which he had, of course, lugged along—the boys saw their opportunity.

Some forward-looking publicity man—they didn't as yet call them public relations vice presidents—got the brilliant idea of telephoning a friend in the sports department of the *Detroit News*. The young writer was extremely skeptical, but took a chance and carted his heavy camera equipment out to Belle Isle.

And it happened again. Only, this time, with bigger potentials than were offered by Lake Pepin or White Bear.

The Detroit River, the boundary between Canada and the United States, was a boundary for other things, too—a country where the finest bourbon, and especially the finest scotch, was legal and for sale; and a dry United States, which tried to subsist on bootleg whisky and bathtub gin.

Traffic between the two countries all up and down the river was heavy, as Ralph was soon to find out.

But meanwhile he was garnering a little publicity.

The *Detroit News* gave him front-page coverage, with pictures and an interview; and a big feature in the sports section. The discovery made by the young sports writer that an important citizen, a Detroit circuit judge, was part owner of the speed boat livery, and the Dodge Water Cars pulling the crazy Swede on his water skis may, of course, have helped to get that valuable coverage. Anyway, Ralph got it. It brought him enough favorable attention that the company hired him to run one of the new boats.

So once again Ralph Samuelson was on his element—water.

Only what a difference!

Instead of trying to get action out of a venerable pile of junk lugging a clam barge, he was at the helm of a slim speedster that responded instantaneously to the throttle-dodged, cavorted, threw up a beautifully low wake.

Not that Ralph stopped his skiing exhibition just because he was now the skipper of a luxurious boat.

The company became so successful that it opened a branch at Lake Orion, a resort area in resort area conscious Central Michigan.

Ralph went to Lake Orion over the weekends, his monstrous eight-foot skis projecting from the shallow hatch of a borrowed car, little red flags tied to the ends.

He was deadly afraid somebody would ram him, damage those precious sliders. He found a solution.

He got permission to drive a car owned by none less than the part owner, the portly judge himself. Nobody would dare ram him now, for the black car, with the official, shiny gold emblem on the side, had a police siren on top that made a shattering racket on command.

Ralph admitted later, with a wry smile, that he got ungodly satisfaction out of opening that siren to get through the heavy traffic of old State Route 24, even narrower in 1926 than it is now.

He didn't know it then, but Ralph was soon to have several near-brushes with the law, when the wily judge, who realized how reliable Ralph was—a nondrinker, nonsmoker, an expert with boats in any weather—hired him to do more and more of his driving, on land and on the water.

"Some called me a damned sissy—a pantywaist because I didn't drink or smoke—until they saw me on my water skis, doing what none of them dared to do," Ralph recalled. "I didn't have to use my fists to impress people—or drink five martinis before dinner. I used my feet, stuck into the leather straps of my skis. And when I skied alone over clear, clean Lake Orion, clean compared with the Detroit River, I had my share of admirers, especially pretty girls. And that was right up my conceited alley at the time!"

While skiing was Ralph's pride and joy, part of his job was not so pleasant, nor as legal, although with a judge as his boss, what could happen?

Ever since he had tied in with the Belle Isle outfit, Ralph had been witness to smuggling, carried on as blatantly as many other Prohibition Era exploits.

Often Ralph watched while fast boats from Ontario, specifically the city of Windsor, landed right next to the boat livery, unloaded as many as 50 cases of the finest imported whisky, transferred the lot to a truck, which then dashed into town—under police escort!

The police protection, probably bought at high bribery-type rates, was to prevent hijacking along the way by rival gangs!

And the judge? He had many friends—all of them thirsty. Often Ralph's job was to take a group of legal giants over to Sunnyside, Ontario, where they would have their booze parties—real sugar daddies, making whoopee with flappers flaunting beautifully marcelled hairdos, while a gramophone, which had to be cranked frequently, dispensed tempo music for dances like the Charleston and crooner music for love making.

Sometimes the judge would be too busy—probably ruling on some case of hijacked liquor—and his friends went joyriding alone.

But Ralph was always the favorite chauffeur.

He was not infallible—had one or two near misses with disaster.

The "Let's-run-over-to-Canada-and-have-a-real-drink" activities went on at night. And the running lights were held to a minimum.

But the Detroit River, main lifeline between all five Great Lakes from Ontario to Superior, carried heavy traffic to and from Duluth, Milwaukee, Chicago, Detroit, Toledo, Cleveland, Buffalo, and a dozen intermediary ports.

The big freighters were slow, but looked taller than the Mississippi bluffs when they bore down on you at night. Their lights were so high, that at times even Ralph, with his keen sight, mistook them for stars.

But one characteristic all ships had—they threw up huge wakes, especially when they were deep in the water.

More than once, Ralph came so close to being rammed by one of these behemoths that he was rocked by their swells like a cork as he maneuvered his vehicle back to the dry United States.

Going over, the gang was usually noisy in their anticipation; coming back, they were either noisier—or sleeping it off.

"But I never lost one of them," Ralph recalled with satisfaction.

Often it was daylight before he got to his very modest hotel, not too far from the river.

The season ended with Labor Day here, too—and Ralph was without a job.

But not without ideas.

Chester Stuart, with his elevator shoes, had a Model T Roadster—and Ralph knew the way to Florida. The little house he and his father had built was still there at Lantana, although the 10 acres, farther inland, were gone.

So, after many conferences, south they went, the top down all the way, the skis strapped to one fender.

It was during this trip that Ralph became the object of suspicion.

The awkward, eight-foot water skis, longer than the car, were jutting out fore and aft.

Somewhere in a tobacco town in South Carolina, the boys were taking gas—that is, colored gasoline was dribbled out of a glass jar atop a hand pump which filled the container, one gallon at a time.

Leaning against the wall of the garage, a former combination harness and wagon shop, an octogenarian in worn overalls, enjoying his chaw of Mail Pouch, stared—not at the car but at the long pieces of wood, curved at the ends. Slowly he let his old hickory chair tilt forward to get a better view.

"What's them, sonny?" he finally asked, spitting a stream to leeward, fixing Ralph with a suspicious stare.

"Skis, grandpa," said Ralph, sticking a nickel into a newfangled machine that released a bottle of strawberry pop.

"What's skis fer, sonny?"

"Mostly to slide on snow.

"Snow?" Grandpa allowed himself a sympathetic chuckle. "You Yankee foreigners don't know much, do ye?"

"What you mean, grandpa?"

"We hardly get enough snow down here to even see it, so how can you slide on it?"

"But these skis are not for snow."

"But you said…"

"I know. But these skis are to ski on water."

"On what?"

"On water."

"Water?.You mean *water*?"

"Yes."

"You mean, you freeze the water and make it slick, and you slide on it?"

"No, grandpa. Unfrozen water. Like the water you got out in the ocean."

"Water?"

"Right."

"Where you goin' to do this?"

"Florida."

"Aha! That explains it. Lot of damn fool things is done in Florida. But I sure never heard nobody crazy enough to think he could slide on water—even in Florida. I guess—maybe—you're jest a little tetched?"

"Other people have said so, too," admitted Ralph good-naturedly.

"That's what I thought," said grandpa. "You—you ain't plannin' to stay here, I hope?"

"You mean, you don't like crazy people in this town?"

"That's my meanin'."

"Guess I'll have to move on then."

"Good," said grandpa.

But he didn't relax enough to tilt his chair back until Ralph and Chester were back in their car. As they pulled away, Ralph heard grandpa snicker as he talked to the station owner about that "crazy Yank."

"Did you get the name of that filling station?" asked Ralph.

"Yeah. I always write down everything for the record," said Stuart. "Why?"

"Should have given the old geezer a picture of me actually skiing on water. Got some in my bag. Thought I might send him one from Florida. Oh, well—forget it. He'd call the picture a fake anyway—or accuse me of being in league with the Devil himself."

Ralph long wondered what grandpa would have said if he had been confronted with visual evidence that a man can ski on water—even in South Carolina!

22. THE DENTIST

In Lantana, which was still staggering from the blows of the busted land boom, Chester got himself a job in a small restaurant. Ralph thought it rather appropriate that a short man like Chester would become a short-order cook.

Ralph's ambition was more aquatic. And after a bit of waiting he found himself something to his liking—running a fishing boat for a snowbird from Cleveland, spending his winters in Florida.

Allen Cross, dentist, warned by the unsuccessful speculations of friends, had invested more wisely. As a result, he had an imposing home along the shore in Lantana.

He lacked a boathouse. Ralph built him one—on 14-foot piles, forced into the oozing mud by hydraulic pressure, using a homemade contraption, a 2-inch pipe, 10 feet long, connected to a nearby fire hydrant. Ralph had always been good at improvising.

With the help of a third party, tall, easy-going Walter Hagg, they got the pilings in place, fit forms around them, filled them with cement—insurance against the frequent hurricanes.

On top of the pilings they constructed a good boathouse.

Ralph's ingenuity earned him not only Dr. Cross's attention, but that of his granddaughter, blond, lovable, 20-year-old Alice Marie. She insisted on going along on all fishing trips, apparently captivated by the handsome young Swede, who had already demonstrated his courage several times on those weird water skis of his. Alice's mother, Besse, looked on.

Naturally, there was talk of Ralph's past experiences in Detroit, and eventually Dr. Cross wondered why they couldn't start a similar boat livery. He was a promoter at heart, even agreed to finance the deal—starting with two boats.

They found a good location for such a livery, in Palm Beach, near old Highway No. 1, crowded with more tourists every winter. The spot even had a boathouse that could be converted into a terminal for livery boats.

While they were busy cleaning up the place, Besse Michaels, Dr. Cross's married daughter and Alice's mother, came to Ralph in private and asked for an interview.

They met on a deserted part of the beach that night.

"You're a good boy," said Besse, in her somewhat whisky-soaked voice. "I like you; that's why I'm doing this."

"Doing what, Besse?" asked Ralph, wondering if he had been coaxed into an assignation with an older woman.

"Warning you."

"Warning me? What about?"

"Warning you against my father. Sure, I know, it looks lousy, disloyal, me informing against my father. All I say is, look out. Don't invest any money in any company he's connected with."

"But why in the world not, Besse?"

"I'm warning you, is all. I've known him for a long time. Just don't trust him with money. Sorry, but I like you. So does Alice Marie. I don't want you to get hurt, that's all. Don't ever mention this meeting, or I'll deny it."

Ralph was flabbergasted. Was Besse drunk? Didn't seem to be. He decided to disregard the strange warning—whatever it was, especially since Alice Marie was so enthusiastic about the idea of forming a boat leasing company.

Meanwhile Ralph nearly ended his career and that of trusting little Alice Marie.

One day in spring, Ralph had made some minor repairs on Dr. Cross's powerboat and was taking her out for a test spin. At the last moment Alice Marie jumped in.

It could have been the last ride for both of them.

They decided to take the boat out on Lake Worth, a bay of the ocean. A little ways out, Ralph saw a dark shadow in the water and judged it to be a huge shark. With his usual daredevil disregard for danger, he had often annoyed those bandits of the deep by pricking them with his pike.

But the shadow turned out to be a different kind of fish.

Ralph came nearer, prodded at the dark spot as they passed it, expecting the shark to make a splashing, harmless, diving getaway.

The pike and the propeller of the boat didn't disturb a shark this time, but they annoyed the heck out of a giant ray, dozing near the surface.

The ray went into instantaneous action. The boat and its rider went straight up in the air; the tail of the beast, 10 to 12 feet long, and as big around as a man's leg, lashed out with terrific fury; the animal's body, 14 feet wide and about as long, rolled and twisted.

"God must have been with me as he was in my water skiing, because instead of splintering the boat, and stunning us, in which case we would certainly have drowned, the craft landed right-side-up again, half-filled with water, but intact. The motor was killed, but undamaged," Ralph recalled. The ray was gone.

Later that spring, Ralph accompanied the Cross family as far as their home in Cleveland. There they formed a corporation. Dr. Cross was, of course, president and treasurer; Ralph was vice president; Alice Marie became secretary.

Dr. Cross left the choice of boats to Ralph and advanced $2,000, a magnificent sum back in 1926 and 1927. Ralph lost no time, ordered two beautiful Gar Wood boats, 28 feet long, to be delivered to Lantana by freight the following November, 1927.

Chester and Ralph returned to their job under the Belle Isle Bridge in Detroit and got the 12 boats ready for the grand opening, Decoration Day, then May 31.

Once again, Ralph swished into the limelight with his skis by giving water ski exhibitions.

But every time he did, with the scum and refuse of the dirty Detroit River flying about his ears, he longed for the clear water of Lake Pepin.

"But even on the filthy dividing line between Canada and the United States, God tried to speak to me, the thoughtless, unthinking, daredevil water skier," Ralph said.

Several times that summer Ralph came close to understanding that life should be a sacred thing, dedicated to God, not squandered or wasted.

Belle Isle, Ralph discovered, was one of the favorite jumping-off places for Detroit's potential suicide cases.

One afternoon, Chester and he were standing on their dock when it happened again: they saw a hurtling body, heard a big splash in the filthy river.

"Here we go once more," shouted Ralph, jumping into the driver's seat. Chester joined him. They roared to the spot, and Chester jumped overboard to save the victim—a young woman.

This one, as others before her, didn't want to be saved. In fact, she was very energetic about it.

Ralph heard her shriek, "Leave me alone. I want to die!"

"God damn you, leave me alone. To hell with this life. Damn you, let me die."

It shocked Ralph as no previous suicide attempt had. Could a human being actually hate life so much, that she'd curse God while trying to die?

It took the combined strength of both men to get that frantic female into the boat. She scratched, bit, struck out with her fists, cursed everything and everybody, but especially the deity. Chester, his cheeks bleeding, finally hit her over the head with an oar.

"For many nights I heard that woman's curses in my ears," Ralph recalled. "Cursing God at the hour of death! It shocked me. It made me wonder, too. Was there a God at all? If so, what was He, where was He, what was He doing?

"But the feeling passed. I wasn't ready for Him."

For one thing, Ralph had his mind on Alice Marie that summer. She was in Cleveland, he in Detroit, but there was a night steamer between the two points, across lower Lake Erie. Ralph used it frequently—spending weekends with the luscious, cuddly Alice Marie who, so Ralph remembers, "craved affection more than any woman I had ever met."

Both Alice Marie and Ralph were looking forward to fall and winter when they could bask in the Florida sun—together again.

They encountered a delay.

A brutal hurricane struck Florida. Word reached Cleveland that the Cross house was hit hard.

Ralph and Stuart jumped into the Model T, huffed and puffed practically nonstop to Florida.

They found chaos.

The doctor's beautiful house had 10 inches of mud in it; the doctor's car, which he always left in Florida, required a complete overhaul to correct the damage done by saltwater. Trees were down; the Lantana bridge across the Lake Worth entrance had vanished completely. At Palm Beach, nothing was left of the buildings they had leased for their boat livery but a few battered pilings sticking incongruously out of the now deceptively calm water.

The doctor's boathouse at Lantana was one of the few structures that had weathered the storm. Ralph's pilings had held. But the boat inside was junk.

The little house Ralph and his father had built was roofless. The shores of Lake Worth were lined with smashed boats.

"I learned two things from that hurricane, which I didn't experience in person, although I certainly saw the aftermath," Ralph philosophized. "First, I asked, why did a compassionate God do this to mankind? Was it punishment? Or wasn't there a God at all? Perhaps all this was a natural phenomenon, and God had nothing to do with it. Or, perhaps, he wasn't a compassionate God at all? Perhaps he was the cruel God. I suddenly remembered what old Reverend Peterson was always yelling about, according to my parents who used him to scare me at times.

"Yes, in my simple, naive, almost childish way, immature and groping, I actually began to think of God. It was a new experience—a disturbing one.

"Secondly, I learned that human beings have fantastic rebounding capacities. I marveled at the way people in that area came out of their misery.

"I wondered—were people more God-like than I had given them credit for? Was there a bit of divine courage and strength in all of us, whether we knew it or not?

"I also learned something else even more disturbing. I didn't have answers to any of my questions.

"Not then.

"And not for a long time."

23. ON ONE FOOT

Ralph and his group had to start all over again—with new pilings, new planks, a whole new boat livery dock.

Their labor force had been enlarged by one Dick Flay.

During this time of travail and uncertainly, there was one compensation. Ralph had an opportunity to display his skill on water skis, something he loved to do above everything else. The

"Oh's" and "Ah's" and the applause of spectators on shore as he whizzed by meant as much to him as the applause of a theatre audience to a professional actor or speaker.

Most of Ralph's skiing was done during the intermissions of National and International Boat Races.

"In those days I couldn't even visualize water shows as they exist today, when the main attraction is usually a complicated display of tricks and skills by skiing groups," Ralph said. "I was all alone—the only freak on boards.

"But this I know. Lot of people from all parts of the world were present at those exhibitions. There's no doubt in my mind that some French sports enthusiasts took the idea back to their native France.

"Had I been a little more worldly-wise, I probably would have anticipated that. I didn't. Consequently, for many years, the world was told a Frenchman had invented skiing on water—until a man in New York state made a similar claim—and later one in Seattle. Then, I came along and spoiled it for all of them by proving that I had preceded them all. But that's another story. We'll come to it."

It was at this time that Ralph Samuelson became the inventor of another ski trick—scooting along on one ski!

"I shouldn't claim any credit for that one," said Ralph modestly. "It was an accident.

"I was skiing behind a pretty fast boat—don't remember whose—when I hit the wake thrown up by a large yacht. It ripped off one of my foot straps, the left one. But, instead of falling, I managed to finish the exhibition on one ski.

"The applause was tremendous. I didn't have time to explain that I hadn't done the stunt intentionally. Anyway, nobody asked me.

"After that, I often skied on one foot."

Another stunt didn't end quite as happily. Ralph, remembering Walter Bullocks's old water plane, tried it again, on the ocean, behind another seaplane.

This time, however, he took a bad spill at 75 miles an hour, when he crossed the wake of a ferry boat four times as big as the good old "Verana" on good old Lake Pepin.

Ralph did a complete somersault. But, as he put it, "All I got was some sore muscles. I was back on the water in two days."

The boat livery was a success.

The two Gar Wood boats, powered by marine motors, shoved the hulls of fine Philippine mahogany through the water at 50 miles an hour.

The boats were always in demand—by rich playboys, rich widows, even foreign royalty. One youngster, a European prince only 10 years old, went out daily with his nurse, for four hours or more, at $25 an hour. One countess from Paris took a boat out three hours, 10 days in a row, a total of 30 hours. Sometimes she had a man with her, and Ralph kept his eyes strictly forward. Anyway, her big roll of $100 bills never seemed to get smaller.

Most of the business was done at Palm Beach, some 15 miles north of Lantana. But the beautiful boats were vulnerable to the ruthless, stealthy, and hungry marine enemy, the saltwater borers that ate mahogany as if it were juicy pine.

Every morning, the boats had to be driven north to Palm Beach for business; every night, they had to be driven back again to Lake Worth where the boys had rigged up a "railroad" so they could pull their prize possessions out of the salty sea and rinse them off with sweet water.

Ralph didn't mind. The vice president of the Cross Boat Livery, and its secretary, Alice Marie, who rode along every single day—both ways—conducted business on board, especially on moonlit nights.

Whether it was company business, private business, or monkey business, or a little of each, Ralph would not divulge, nor are there any witnesses. That Alice Marie craved affection he already admitted.

She got it.

In fact, the two were making long-range plans for the future, including marriage, after the $2,000 owed to Dr. Cross would be paid off, and they'd have more facilities, more boats, more drivers.

"But Providence can change our lives when we least expect it. I was soon to learn what Besse Michaels meant when she warned me about getting involved with her father, Dr. Cross," Ralph reminisced wryly. "I had to learn the hard way. The very hard way!"

24. THE ACCIDENT

It was early March 1927.

Ralph, age 24, full of hope and dreams and ambition; Alice Marie, beautiful, some years younger, adoring the man who could do what none had done, ski on one foot on water, among other things; Chester Stuart, the man with the elevator shoes, always doing something; brooding Dick Flay; the calculating Dr. Cross—all were certain Florida would soon have the finest boat livery in the country.

First, Ralph wanted to improve the company office facilities, and the rest rooms out on the dock, by installing running water.

The city water main was under the blacktop road, some 20 feet from the foot of the 150-foot long pier.

Between the pier and the road lay soft, sandy soil, over which the previous owner had laid a crude sidewalk of wooden planks, nailed together into a platform, about 10 feet wide.

The boys decided they'd have to lift that platform high enough to allow them to dig a trench under it, so the new pipes leading to the rest rooms could be laid properly.

They got extra help—managed to hoist that monster of nailed-together planks, and set it on end. They braced it with several 2x4s.

To be safe, Ralph and Chester reinforced the braces with their own backs, while Dick Flay, who had been coaxed away from a card game with Dr. Cross, was to do the actual digging of a two-foot-deep trench.

Everything went as planned—at first. Dick was down on his knees in the trench, digging away with a rusty spade.

Suddenly a heavy gust of wind caught the platform like a sail—just enough to release the braces, let them fall free. The 800 pounds of that platform came bearing down on the backs of Chester Stuart and Ralph Samuelson.

Chester panicked first. "My God—I can't hold her," he wheezed. "I can't hold the damned thing."

"Don't drop it," shouted Ralph, "Dick! Dick—get out of there! Get out of the trench! She's coming down. Hurry, man!"

No doubt Chester did his best, but it was too much for him. He leaped free, letting go his hold.

Ralph tried to do the impossible all by himself. Almost did. He held that platform with his back long enough for Dick Flay to scramble out of the trench on all fours, and roll aside, while the platform finally came crashing down, inches from his head.

While Chester stood around flexing his sore muscles, while Dick Flay stood there, speechless, Ralph Samuelson lay on the sand, writhing in agony.

Alice Marie came running. "What's wrong?" she exclaimed. "What's wrong, Ralph? I saw it all. It was wonderful. Dick, Ralph just saved your life, you know that? He saved your life. Come, help me. Something's happened to him."

Something had indeed happened to Ralph Samuelson.

He had broken his back.

A compression fracture, doctors called it later.

Little was known about broken backs in those days. Ralph went to bed stayed there for several weeks. Friends suggested a chiropractor; the pre-physical therapy gentleman didn't help much.

While lying in bed in Lantana, almost immobile, his back one horrid agony, other troubles were piling up.

The two streamlined boats, with their powerful motors, were under warranty—on condition they'd be lubricated with a special kind of oil prescribed by the manufacturer.

Whether it was Dr. Gross, or Chester, who fell for the fast talk of a visiting oil salesman, nobody would ever discover. But one of them bought inferior oil.

This raised utter havoc with the sensitive motors. They heated up until the pistons stuck and then went right through the crankcase—first in one boat, then in the other. Chester's boat even caught fire.

"My tribulations were really beginning in earnest," said Ralph. "Here I had been riding high, ready to get married to a bewitching girl—oh, yes, they were going to take me into the family, and I was willing and eager.

"Now here I was in bed, with a broken back, no boats, no job, nothing."

What to do? Detroit was out. Ralph couldn't even stand up, much less drive a fast boat for rum runners.

The answer, as so often in the lives of human beings when they are in trouble, was to go home!

So Ralph went home, Chester doing the driving.

In Lake City, Ralph was welcomed like a lost son by the entire family.

But Ralph couldn't miss it. There were those in town who snickered and nodded with that "I told you so" satisfaction.

Ralph's broken back was not caused by water skiing. It had happened on the dry sand of a Florida beach, not on water. It had happened because he was thinking of others, not himself. That didn't stop the gossips from drawing their own, convenient conclusions about the Lake City water skier some thought the "conceited ham."

Hardly had Ralph been home two months, now hobbling around a bit, when word came that Dr. Cross had died of a heart attack while watching an air show in Cleveland.

With the assistance of Ben, his brother, Ralph made the train journey to Cleveland. When he got there—more bad news.

Ralph was advised by a lawyer that Dr. Cross had squandered every penny of the fund Ralph had sent him to pay off the new boats!

Nothing was left to make even one payment, or to try to get the damaged boats repaired.

"I never went back to Florida, never saw Alice Marie again. It all proved to be just a memory. And soon people forgot me and my water skiing, too!"

With these 29 words, laconic, hiding whatever bitterness he felt, Ralph Samuelson summed up a whole segment of his life, his love, his career.

And the man whose life he had saved at the expense of his own wealth, health, and future?

He disappeared.

The whole world had come crashing down around Ralph Samuelson's ears.

After a few more weeks, with the pain in his back getting no better, Ralph finally went to the family doctor in Lake City, and eventually to a clinic in Red Wing for X-rays.

"When can I ski again?" Ralph asked after one of these visits.

"Ski? You want to ski on those unstable boards of yours?" exclaimed the doctor. "Ralph, are you—I mean, you're lucky you can even walk with this compression fracture. You'll never water ski again. Never. Unless you want to break your back completely, and be paralyzed for the rest of your life."

It was a harsh sentence. Ralph couldn't refute the X-rays. He forgot about water skiing, and settled for just plain walking—on land.

If life is a series of peaks and valleys, Ralph Samuelson had slid into a very deep, deep valley ... without the benefit of his skis.

The fantastic, eight-foot long boards, which he had religiously brought back to Lake City, where they had been born, were stuck away on the rafters of the old Samuelson boathouse, next to the two-holer. There they lay until Ralph had his own home, when they were again stuck on rafters, this time in a barn.

The skis were not to be rediscovered until 21 years later. Ralph himself wouldn't be lifted out of anonymity until 15 years after that—a total of 36 years.

"Meanwhile God was to test me further—often—at times almost beyond my endurance, or so I thought," said Ralph, "until I was a regular Job on water skis, all right without the water skis. I was Job in the dust of Minnesota. And at the time I didn't even realize it was God giving me the works."

25. THE STORM

His pockets empty, his back broken, with no job, Ralph Samuelson once more looked to the Lake for help.

And the Lake, which had been kind to him so often in the past—which one day was to become even more famous because of him—suggested one quiet day in early summer, "Why not go back to clamming? You still have your equipment. Your brother, Donald, will help you, and you can do as much as your back allows. Come on! Spend some time on me again! I'll soothe your jangled nerves, relax your tense, injured spine. I'll give you the peace and comfort and companionship you've been missing as the months roll by."

Ralph heard, understood, acted.

Donald, two years younger than Ralph, had rented a small wooden shack down in the lower part of town—by the Lake, of course. Ralph moved in with him.

The southern part of Lake City was an enigma, an area of contrast. It had a few low-brow shanties, some garages, discarded sheds, junky dumps.

But only half a mile farther south was located a mansion in all its Victorian gingerbread splendid, glass and glitter and glory, surrounded by acres of formal, cultivated gardens, a small golf course. It had a swimming pool, a majestic dock, yachts, sailboats, motorboats, guest houses, riding stables, ice houses, and greenhouses. It had porches and scores of guest rooms, servants' quarters and gazebos, and a 90-foot flagpole. It was known for its parties, banquets, dances, its hilarity and all around money-defying luxury.

That complex was the showpiece of Lake City. Captains floating by on their luxurious packets pointed it out to their excursioning passengers. It even had a name—Pepin Lodge.

Exclusive it was—with a fence around it. And exclusive were the people living there. Rich. Nobody knew how rich. Nobody knew how C.K. Berkey had made his money. Rumors had it he made "uncounted millions" annually in Chicago, in the egg-carton business.

It was all far beyond the horizon of Ralph Samuelson, self-acknowledged poor boy.

Oh, he had publicity, had considered himself important, had swelled with pride when he saw his pictures in the sports sections of newspapers—whipping along on water skis, a handsome daredevil.

But that was all behind him.

He was an invalid, at least a semi-invalid. Although his back was mending enough for him to walk, he still had to be extremely careful.

So the Berkeys, whose house he could see through the bushes and trees around Donald's shack, who he could hear, sometimes until dawn, were as unreachable as—as skiing again.

Then, once more, it was the Lake that came to Ralph's rescue, this time not in a gentle, coaxing, consoling mood, but in one of her angry tantrums.

A summer storm, which only Midwesterners can really appreciate, came down on them.

It was a dandy! Ralph and Donald were sleeping in an old army tent as they liked to do. That temporary domicile simply took off right over their heads. Garbage cans followed, flying tree limbs beat tattoos on flying wash tubs as they met in mid-air.

Ralph's first thought was of their boats, some 500 feet out in the Lake.

But they were well anchored in a cove, and were riding it out.

Farther down the shore, however, things were different.

The Berkey boats, either more exposed or probably less expertly anchored, were dragging their hooks. Every time they were visible in one of the long flashes of lightning, they seemed closer to annihilation as they were driven nearer the rocks of a projecting cliff.

Lake Pepin was challenging the rich Berkeys, and winning.

Ralph remembered that the Berkey caretaker, one Ben Buckley, lived on the other side of town.

Soon, weaving searchlights were focused on the dock as the Pepin Lodge household became aware of the danger to their precious playthings, their boats. Ralph could see lights bobbing up and down—lanterns carried by the frantic owners.

But the boats kept drifting away, ghostly in the faint flicker of the spotlights, silhouetted against more intense flashes of weirdly bluish-white lightning.

Ralph could never turn down a dare. And it seemed his Lake was daring him now.

"What in tarnation you think you're doing?" exclaimed Donald, when Ralph got into his bathing suit as fast as his back permitted.

"Can't let those boats drift. They'll be smashed."

"You're going out there?"

"Sure. Looks like fun," said Ralph.

"But your back!"

"This may do it good. Come on, be a sport. Row me to the 'Gosoon'."

"Can't get through that surf."

"We've gotten through worse. Let's get 'agittin', please, Don?"

Ralph could be very persuasive—and forceful. Donald gave in. Their rowboats were nearly swamped before they made it, but after a few spills the two potential boat-savers got past the breakers. Ralph climbed into his small launch, the "Gosoon," got the motor going, and took out after Berkey's two runaway boats.

Waiting for more lightning flashes to help him, Ralph managed to pull alongside the big yacht. The two brothers attached a line to her from the launch, released the bigger craft's useless anchor.

Opening the "Gosoon's" throttle, the two Samuelsons managed to pull "Pepin Lodge I" up the Lake to the safer harbor area. Then returned to rescue the sailboat, almost on the rocks by now and dragged it to the harbor, too.

Ralph and his Lake had never had more fun!

26. PEPIN LODGE

As in all good success-follows-good-deed stories of the time, including *McGuffey's Readers*, virtue was rewarded.

It began the next day.

Mr. Berkey sent word he wanted to see Ralph who bristled a little, thinking the rich man might be condescending and offer him a small reward, something he felt was beneath his dignity. He went.

Berkey thanked the young man graciously for risking his life—then politely asked if he'd like to work for him. Duties: take charge of the running of their large yacht, "Pepin Lodge II," which wasn't on Lake Pepin at the moment, as well as "Pepin Lodge I," the one he had saved, the sailboat, some motorboats, take care of the swimming pool—that sort of thing.

By this time, they were surrounded by the small, lively Berkey children—June, Peter, Andy, and Johnnie, all admiring the hero of the storm.

It was partly the kids who induced Ralph to take the job. "And the pay was satisfactory, too," Ralph recalled, understating as he often did.

A different life began for Ralph Samuelson. The young fellow who had piloted friends of rum runners, who had won a certain acclaim as a daring water skiier, who had dreamed of marrying a beautiful blonde and running a boat livery in Florida, was now an employee of a rich man.

He even had an expense account to buy the kids whatever they wanted, was given carte blanche to do shopping, was in complete charge of all vehicles with the Berkey brand, be they on land or on water.

Ralph soon proved his reliability. For one thing, he could always be trusted to bring the most happy party of whoopee-makers back safely from a lake or river trip, because he never touched the stuff.

Besides, he could repair ships and cars, and do things nobody else could, it seemed.

For instance, C.K. had installed a water vacuum pump to clean out the big pool by suction. It had never worked right. Ralph discovered why. The motor was wired wrong, running backward and shoving dirt into the pool, instead of sucking it out.

Ralph also took a fantastic chance with his back. He made like a steeplejack with a series of half-hitches and a steeplejack's seat, somewhat like a boatswain chair, and hoisted himself to the pinnacle of that 90-foot flagpole and painted it from the top down—after once dropping a bucket of paint, creating a splotched white circle flyers could have used as a landmark.

Ralph, in short, always did what needed doing, like recovering a chest of family silver some exuberant visitor had gleefully tossed overboard, or retrieving the bicycles that had been alcoholically ridden into the pool the night before.

Decades later June Berkey, a svelte, sophisticated young matron, still living half the year in one of the houses on the estate—the so-called River House not too far from the now unoccupied lodge—remembered those days as some of the happiest of her life.

She hadn't met Ralph for over 40 years when he called on her to renew old friendships. They had a wonderful time reminiscing. June recalled especially how much they had missed Ralph when he finally left them to get married.

"The man who took your place only made us realize all the more what we had in you," she told Ralph in her unique home, the reception room displaying June's love and respect for owls, for it has at least 100 different replicas of the wise bird, from the finest Swedish crystal to wooly white ones.

"Your successor," she chuckled, "was a German. On the first trip out on the yacht, father ordered him to throw out the anchor. He did—rope and all. We had to retrieve the gear by diving for it. He didn't last long."

June, oldest of the four Berkey children, remembered what a friend Ralph had always been. "To this day we have deep affection for him," said June, who became Mrs. W.C. D'Arcy and spent her winters in Florida near where Ralph used to water ski.

While visiting, the two also recalled another family crisis. June's mother, Clarice, later living in California, had bought two expensive ceramic planters in Palm Beach and had lugged them home. Ralph was to take them in the station wagon to the same Jewell Nursery where he used to pull those millions of weeds.

On the way back, one of the planters tipped over and broke into many pieces. Mrs. Berkey was inconsolable. Ralph fixed that, too, somehow glued the pot together. When he visited June more than four decades later, he found the planter still intact, bearing red geraniums.

While working for the Berkeys, Ralph decided he had to have a new car. Not just any car, but a cream-colored, trimmed-in-brown Ford cabriolet one-seater, with a rumble seat, a gas tank under the dash that could be shut off with the foot, simulating an out-of-gas situation. But the girls of Lake City, Red Wing, Wabasha, and Winona soon caught on and warned each other.

There were other adventures. Ralph was taking one of the Berkey yachts into harbor near the government pier, close to the spot where today a grateful city, state, and nation have placed a commemorative plaque in honor of the Father of Water Skiing.

There was no such plaque that summer day when the Lake City Fire Department unsuccessfully grappled for a drowned man.

Berkey and Ralph both plunged into the deep, dredged-out area, and recovered the body—too late to save him.

That attempt to save a man's life—even as he had saved men and women under the Belle Isle Bridge and as he had saved a man's life in Florida—proved that Ralph's back was well enough to permit diving.

But the pain was always there. He still didn't dare try skiing. Every doctor warned him against it.

And then Fate stepped in again, stepped on Ralph's heart. In his cream-colored cabriolet, in a place known as Oak Center, 10 miles inland, less than an hour away.

The thriving little milk-butter-and-cream hamlet loved to sponsor dances in its barnlike municipal hall.

One Saturday night, Ralph met Marilyn O'Casey, a farmer's daughter, a rich farmer's daughter, whose parents owned and operated a 320-acre farm and rented another near Zumbro Falls, Oak Center's neighbor.

Said Ralph simply, "I left the job at the Berkeys, and we were married on July 4, 1932."

It was 10 years and two days since Ralph had first succeeded in water skiing and 29 years and one day since he was born.

Fourth of July firecrackers came in handy for a noisy shivaree, on the night before the wedding, Ralph's birthday.

"Until death do us part," said Marilyn and Ralph in a simple ceremony held in the bride's home near Zumbro Falls.

"Until death do us part!"

They didn't wait that long.

"Our marriage lasted for 15 years," said Ralph. "Until 1947. Then God really made a Job out of me!"

Minnesota Historical Society

Ralph Samuelson zipped toward a shore filled with thousands who watched the Lake Pepin daredevil demonstrate the water sport he invented July 2, 1922.

Courtesy of Lake City Graphic

Ralph Samuelson (holding his 1920s skis), and Lake City Harbor Master and beach promoter Ben Simons, celebrated Samuelson's world recognition as the Father of Water Skiing in 1966.

Ralph Samuelson became the world's first speed skier when he traveled up to 80 mph behind a World War I Curtis Flying Boat in August 1925.

Minnesota Historical Society

Ruechert's Hardware, in 1923-24, where the Father of Water Skiing purchased the 100 feet of sash cord that tied him to the motorboat the day he invented water skiing, July 2, 1922.

Baesher's Harness Shop, in 1923-24, where Ralph Samuelson obtained the leather to make the foot straps of the world's first water skis.

Lake City photos by Otto Voightlander. Source: Lake City Graphic

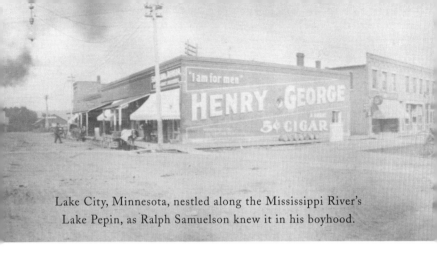

Lake City, Minnesota, nestled along the Mississippi River's
Lake Pepin, as Ralph Samuelson knew it in his boyhood.

Collin's Drug Store, in 1923-34, where Ralph Samuelson's old skis were first publicly displayed by Ben Simons during the 1948 Water Carnival.

Jane's Sweet Shop, in 1923-24, where young fisherman, Ralph Samuelson, enjoyed banana splits.

Jewell Nursery, in 1923-24, where Lake City boys, including the Samuelson brothers, pulled weeds to supplement their families' incomes.

The *Lake City Graphic* newspaper staff is pictured in 1923-24, at the time they were first covering the water antics of local daredevil Ralph Samuelson.

Downtown Lake City as it appeared during Ralph Samuelson's childhood. Featured is the Lyon Hotel as it appeared in 1916.

The Wisconsin Pearl Button Company was one of several Lake City businesses that prospered from the clamming business Ralph Samuelson's family took part in.

Lake City photos by Otto Voightlander. Source: Lake City Graphic

Bob Parrott, Lake City Graphic

Charlene Wold, Water Carnival Queen in 1966, accepted her first pair of water skis from the Father of Water Skiing, Ralph Samuelson.

The December 1949 issue of the Minnesota Turkey Growers Association's magazine featured Ralph Samuelson's turkey farming innovations.

Minnesota Turkey Growers Association

The Father of Water Skiing was immortalized in a stamp issued by the tiny island of Davaar in 1972 to mark water skiing's 50th anniversary.

Courtesy of Allen Bubolz

Courtesy of Lucy Sontag

Ralph Samuelson's water skiing legacy was apparent in Lake City where the Ski Gulls ski team performed in the 1970s.

Ralph Samuelson helped dedicate a plaque erected near the shores of Lake Pepin to mark the 50th anniversary of water skiing in 1972.

Minnesota Historical Society

In 1976, one year before his death, Ralph Samuelson helped unveil a wave statue on the shores of Lake Pepin.

Courtesy of Carolyn McCormick

Beginning July 2, 1922, the Father of Water Skiing, Ralph Samuelson, left a wake for all other skiers to follow.

Minnesota Historical Society

{5}

Section

27. A WIFE

Marilyn O'Casey was Irish, of course, dark-haired, with moonstone eyes, sexy movements, a plump bosom she carried braless, swinging hips, and loving arms that could cling.

If Fickle Fate ever played tricks on man, it played them on Ralph Samuelson when it transplanted him from his beloved Lake, where he was king, to a farm tucked away between the ravines and hills of the crooked Zumbro River, miles from Highway 63, accessible only by one narrow, winding lane, so tortuous only cows felt at home on it.

And there, on the farm that Marilyn's father had put at their disposal, in a house spacious enough but poorly furnished, unpainted, hardly snow-proof, with a roof that needed repair, the small-town boy tried to be a small-time farmer—a peasant.

At first, love made everything seem wonderful. Marilyn and Ralph shared things, dreamt together, starved together, and slept together whenever the flesh moved them.

Of course, with hindsight, it lost much of its glamour.

Ralph summed it up nostalgically later: "This marriage to sexy Marilyn O'Casey taught me a good lesson: never select a wife for your lifelong mate unless you have prayed about it first.

"A woman can look beautiful, be very sexy, but it takes character to keep a marriage together. It takes character, stamina, courage, and humility on the part of both man and wife."

Not that Ralph and Marilyn didn't display some strength of character in the beginning.

For one thing, Ralph, who had no Christian background—at least no personal Christian background—joined the Zumbro Falls church of his wife.

It was the time of the Great Depression, which had crept up on a happy-go-lucky nation like a wolf on the fold, until millions were out of work, looking for jobs, some looking for scraps of food.

Ralph and Marilyn didn't go hungry, although the first winter was a vintage one. The young couple were snowbound for weeks on end, could get out only on skis. Ralph had to cut wood for the fair-sized heating stove and the kitchen range. There were plenty of dead trees around the place; but at 50 below zero, fires must blaze all night, and wood burns faster than coal.

When staples got low, they put on their snow skis and managed to get to the old corner store at Zumbro Falls, load a gunny sack with necessities, flour, sugar, coffee, salt, thread, soap, and baking soda, and lug it home.

They had raised their own pig and butchered that for meat. Their own cow gave them milk, although Marilyn had to do the milking. Ralph, the city slicker, never learned how.

All the time, Ralph had to worry about his back. If he moved wrong, or too fast, the pain became excruciating. But he learned to live with it—often in agony.

Ralph borrowed a combination fox-and-coon dog from his brother-in-law, and spent many nights down along the Zumbro, hunting coons. He sold the pelts for a few dollars each; fox skins brought more. He shot pheasants and partridges for food.

But slowly, as the honeymoon waned, one implacable enemy came to live with them—boredom.

Whether the boredom of those winters out on the isolated farm contributed to what happened to Ralph's marriage later, nobody knows. It may well have left its effects.

The first thaws of spring released them, permitted them to use the winding lane out of their isolation. Because it was still too muddy to use the fancy car, Ralph hitched up their young mare, named Brownie for obvious reasons—just to get away for awhile. Both climbed into the old top buggy, which had lost its top.

The road was not only muddy; it was hilly.

Brownie, still skittish from a winter of inactivity, pranced too exuberantly. The back strap under the horse's belly, intended to keep the buggy from getting too close to her heels, broke.

The buggy rammed right into Brownie's sensitive hind legs. She took off down the first hill as fast as she could go, Ralph yelling, "Whoa—whoa—whoa you beast," and jerking the reins. They made the first curve, but it was too much for Marilyn. She jumped out over the back, landed on her stomach in the mud.

Ralph was still bracing his feet against the floorboards, rotten floorboards it turned out. They gave way, dropping him so he straddled the reach. Now he couldn't even jump had he wanted to.

They made the second curve, a vicious one. Up ahead, Ralph saw a tree he remembered, with a wide crotch. Somehow he managed to yank the reins so hard that he forced the frantic Brownie to leap right into it.

"Believe me, she stuck fast and never went another foot. Nothing was left of the old buggy and the harness, of course. But miraculously, I wasn't hurt," says Ralph." I had to go back home, get an axe to cut one of the limbs off, to get that mare free."

Marilyn was scratched up a bit, but wasn't seriously hurt.

Only Ralph's ego received a bruising wallop. Together they rode the horse back, Marilyn's arms around her husband's stomach.

There were other experiences—especially one when Ralph was helping his 10-year-old brother-in-law to bend a piece of iron by heating it red-hot in a homemade forge, set up, foolishly, in the barn.

When he hit the iron on the improvised anvil he had rigged up, a spark flew toward the ceiling where Ralph's father-in-law had stored a bag of powder to blast stumps.

Blasting powder will blast only when confined; but it will produce the most spectacular fireworks when loose and touched off, as it was in this case.

The two got out of that barn in a hurry. By a miracle, it didn't catch fire. "I was beginning to think I must be leading a charmed life," said Ralph.

But, by this time, Ralph Samuelson had realized that farming the rolling acres in the Zumbra Valley, be it ever so historic, simply did not appeal to him.

The daredevil in him was restless.

He and Marilyn talked it over. She was amenable to anything.

Ralph decided to do what some of his wife's relatives were trying to do—raise turkeys. He was sure he could do it better.

He did … for many years.

28. SORROW

Before Ralph could maneuver himself into his new profession of raising turkeys—for profession it turned out to be—he was struck by personal sorrow, right in the solar plexus.

Ralph's mother died in the fall of 1933.

It was a sad September day when they buried her on the family plot in Lake City's Lakewood Cemetery, near the old oak, hundreds of years old.

"My mother, Mary, was never one to complain," Ralph said after the funeral. "She never grumbled about ill health or talked about her troubles. The woman who went into the weaving business to keep her growing family together, who had worked long, weary hours to provide for us, who had borne six children and had seen two of them buried, now was laid to rest next to her little Charlie who had bled to death, and little Clarence who died at the age of two.

"She always shared all my problems, and also my success, joyfully, when I finally skied on water. But when she became ill of ulcers, she didn't whimper. She was of very rugged Swedish stock.

"She could be very strict with us, and knew how to use the willow when necessary. However, I never regretted her discipline. I'm sure we needed it.

"When I left her grave, I felt a grievous, personal loss. I wept openly. I felt crushed."

Eventually, life took over again with new challenges. And Ralph Samuelson could never turn down a challenge.

29. THE TURKEYS

Refusing to listen to the warnings of friends, Ralph bought a cheap little hot water incubator, heated by kerosene lamps, and began his new pioneering venture.

He had no particular talent for raising poultry, but corrected his mistakes as he went along, learned from errors, and eventually built up a fair-sized flock of gobblers.

He bought a Jamesway incubator that would hold up to 5,000 eggs. The man who sold it to him, C.J. Thies, became a lifelong friend.

Raising turkeys, bronze or white, in Minnesota, or anywhere, is as much a science as an art. At times it's a game in which Lady Luck holds the winning cards.

What Ralph Samuelson—former water skier, daredevil, exhibitionist, the man with the broken back—learned about turkeys in the next few years would fill a book, which Ralph promised never to try to write.

First he learned the rudiments: The hatching process takes

25 to 28 days; a breeding flock consists of a mature male bird, at least six months old, and 10 hens; from the time they're six weeks old, until they're six months, turkeys are put out on the range. Day-old turkeys are called poults, and remain poults until they're a month old. Poults must be kept under heat battcries, or under brooder stoves, representing the mother hens, for three weeks, until they're big enough to live without artificial heat.

Broiler turkeys are considered ready for market when they reach eight pounds. Broilers can be white-feathered birds, as the feathers mature faster for dressing than those of bronze turkeys, who have too many dark pinfeathers.

Turkeys have to be kept immaculately clean, since they are very susceptible to diseases. The type of ground feed they get is important. It must include whole grain, such as corn and wheat.

It takes many buildings to raise turkeys. The breeder house for the hens, who produce the eggs, must be kept at a constant temperature of 50 degrees, even in subzero winter weather—not a small achievement. Egg production can be increased by turning on artificial lights early in the morning to create a longer day for the easily misled turkeys.

The birds on the range can fall victim to foxes, owls, and rattlesnakes. An owl can swoop down, take off a turkey's head at one pass, and then fly away with it and eat it.

More than 1,000 facts like that had to be learned. Ralph did his best to master them, bizarre as some of them were.

And as he learned the ABCs of the turkey mystery, his ambition grew, feeding on itself.

He needed more land, preferably nearer Mazeppa, a neighboring town, larger than Zumbro Falls.

Ralph found a place with a house and barn and 47 acres of land. He bought the whole thing with a contract for deed, as his funds were still limited—severely.

The house was a small, one-story building with two bedrooms, bath and living room, dining room and small kitchen. It lay somewhat protected in a romantic hollow, facing hills, prairie, and woods. The river valley wasn't too far away.

Ralph, persuasive as always, managed to get several good-sized loans, and in the next few years added building after building, especially a big, two-story plant to house incubators.

He became as tenacious a pioneer in raising turkeys as he had been a tenacious pioneer in water skiing.

"I conceived the idea that if I had a building large enough to hold a big flock of breeder hens, we could perhaps get even better and bigger results.

"So I became a pioneer in housing turkey hens for early egg production," Ralph recalled.

Again C.J. Thies, the incubator salesman who also represented a building firm, came to his assistance. So Ralph's turkey farm boasted a fine modern, well-insulated building, covered with metal, inside and out, equipped with steel doors. It housed a feed room and furnace room, a room to store feed, had fuel-burning floor brooders, two in each pen, big enough to put 200 poults under.

Ralph's building could house 2,800 birds until they were six weeks old, ready to go out on the range!

More than 1,000 turkey hens could be kept active with time clocks that would produce artificial light for 12 hours. Turkey farmers came from far and near to inspect this fabulous new plant.

Then Ralph had to have another building to house another incubator, 80 feet long and 40 wide, with a furnace room, and an entrance wide enough to drive a special panel truck inside, and load the day-old poults under a dry roof.

Soon, Ralph was raising turkeys for market and, at the same time, making a business of poults, until he sometimes sold 3,000 day-old, baby turkeys a week.

He had hatching capacity for 50,000 eggs with automatic

turning devices to simulate the trampling mother hen.

As Ralph summed it up years later, "We became very successful in our turkey venture and made a good return on our investment." Another typical understatement.

Those were the days when Ralph and Marilyn would occasionally get away to Canada for deer hunting or fishing. They still enjoyed each other's company, still liked the same things. But Ralph never seemed to be able to slow down. He bought more land, raised much of his own feed, hired help to farm his increasing acres, rolling away in the distance.

He used hired help for the farm, but his turkeys he trusted to no one.

In summer, his huge turkey flocks billowed over the hillsides like mysterious white and bronze waves, slowly moving along as the birds grazed on young grass, barley and oats.

Many a night, Marilyn and Ralph spent not in their comfortable beds, but out in a small, wooden, emergency shed, like shepherds of old keeping watch over their flocks.

There they bedded down on hard cots to guard their turkeys, creatures that could get excited easily and gobble like demons. The electrifying gobbling of 10,000 nervous turkeys must be heard to be believed. It's like a spooky, nightmarish sound effect, resembling nothing else in the world. A handclap can set it off.

While the couple chased away foxes, they couldn't cope with the pesky owls.

An owl would dive out of the night, silently and swiftly snap off a turkey's head as if it were made of paper. Instantly the whole flock would stampede, pile up in a corner, and smother each other.

Ralph lost hundreds of valuable birds that way, until he found a way to deal with the night prowlers that came on wings so silent a mouse couldn't hear them.

Ralph doesn't remember who gave him the idea, but he was

told that the predators liked to land on something high near their prey, to look over the situation, before they swooped down for the kill.

After that, whenever Ralph constructed a turkey pen for night lodging of his turkeys, he also erected a thin pole, two inches in diameter, and 10 feet high, with a four by eight inch platform, just large enough for an owl to land on.

But as it did, it got its foot in a trap.

How many owls Minnesota lost that way is not recorded—not too many. But Ralph's losses decreased dramatically.

Those were nights made for love, of course; but too often both partners were too tired for it.

It seemed sex had lost much of its excitement anyway.

By and by, each found some outside activity to compensate. Marilyn joined a choir, an apparently harmless occupation.

Ralph was flying high—not only economically, but physically. He took flying lessons until he could solo at a small airport on the high plateau overlooking historic old Frontenac, not too far from Lake City.

That place was later to play an important role in his life.

Eventually he lost his interest in flying, too. It seemed he was getting jaded more quickly, and more and more often about more and more activities.

Ralph went in for speedboat racing, purchased two luxury boats. One was a B class that made up to 55 miles an hour; the other a C class that could do 65.

He raced them for several seasons, until during a 12-boat race on Lake Pepin, his boat left the water, turned over, dumped him. The motor still running at high speed with its exhaust ports wide open and took water into the cylinder heads, until the whole thing exploded into bits and pieces.

Ralph thought it a good time to quit boat racing. He was bored with it, anyway. Besides, in two years, he had squandered more than $5,000 on broken propellers and minor repairs alone.

"I couldn't understand myself at the time. I had started with nothing—had become a success. I had made more money on my turkey farm than I had ever anticipated. I had everything—except peace of mind and contentment of soul, that is," Ralph said later.

30. THE QUEST

The turkey business, begun on a shoestring, had become a bonanza. The poor boy who had been happy when he had an extra nickel in his overall pockets, who was thrilled when Zack Nihart bought him a 10-cent banana split, now had a Lincoln Continental, motorboats, a plane, radios, phonographs, equipment and buildings worth hundreds of thousands.

But he had no children. Marilyn had been through a hysterectomy; so that was that.

Said Ralph, still trying to reconstruct that period of his life, "I was beginning to realize more and more that in spite of my success, my flying and racing, my vacationing in Canada, my buildings, my farms, I wasn't happy.

"I realized suddenly, as I'm sure many others like me have done, that it wasn't really success that I craved. I wanted something more. Something! I was actually lonely for something—I knew not what. I had money, practically everything money could buy. But all my rationalizing didn't help. I was always searching for some way to satisfy that strange inner hunger gnawing at my soul."

This frustrating hunger grew until Ralph began to feel insecure, nervous, anxious.

Of course, those were anxious times everywhere in the United States, the world. World War II had made people wonder about their personal values.

Ralph, over-age when Pearl Harbor's "Day of Infamy" burst on the country, and being a producer of food, was not subject to the draft. Whether that made him brood, who knows?

But brood, he did, for years.

Back of his home, small in comparison with the dozen turkey buildings that stretched out for nearly a quarter of a mile, was a gentle slope, shaded by elms, walnuts, maples, with a backdrop of pines.

In summer, that hillside was taken over by aromatic bee balm, wild pinks, scarlet mallow, purple coneflowers, fragrant sweet clover, giant thistles. It was home to bees and Monarch butterflies, especially when they were beginning to migrate south in August.

After a day's work with the turkeys, or tilling the acres harvesting millet, and other grain for his birds, Ralph Samuelson, 44, would go and lie out there—to cool off, more importantly, to think.

"I used to look up at the sky," said Ralph, still wondering what happened to him on those silent, lonely evenings, and "gaze at the stars and the beauty of the heavens.

"It made me realize, as it must have made millions before me realize, that a Power greater than man must be running this universe. There just had to be a creator who planned it all, and kept it running."

Obviously Ralph's feelings were merely those of man universal. Ever since the cave, human beings have wondered where they came from, what they were doing here, where they were going.

But to every man the misery of this soul searching, this self-analysis is new and personal when it comes. The quest for inner peace is always an agonizing experience.

At least it was to Ralph Samuelson.

"I began to wonder," he said ingenuously, "what part I had in this world besides raising a few turkeys for strangers to eat. Certainly God must have made man for more than that. I said to myself, 'If there is a God in heaven, I want to know Him in a mighty way. But how does man find God? How will I ever find Him?'"

"I belonged to a church, went almost every Sunday. But my weekly attendance never brought me one hour, one minute of relief. Never once did the church answer my question about the real God. The sermons were dry, spiritless. I didn't find Him there.

"I looked back on my life, and I realized I had been a sinner. But joining the church had not given me surcease. I felt no different after I joined the church than before, when I was completely godless.

"Obviously, the church was not the answer. So I kept on searching, crying inside, longing for an answer—a sign, any sign."

The sign came—an ugly, painful, shattering one a tragedy that almost ended the career, and the life, of one Ralph Samuelson.

31. THE BETRAYAL

It all began to hang out at a convention of poultry supply manufacturers at Mason City, Iowa, a busy, industrial town in the northern part of the state.

Ralph, now known as a remarkably successful turkey raiser (his water ski escapades had long since been forgotten), and Marilyn were staying in one of the larger hotels, headquarters for many hatchery men and their wives.

Ralph was there for three reasons: to meet some of the manufacturers; to inspect their displays of new equipment, some of which he might need in the future; and to have a good time, and meet friends.

Marilyn was there for one reason—to have a good time.

She did, for a while.

Until she discovered that a certain manufacturing company vice president—who had invited her into his room while Ralph was busy somewhere talking dreary turkey gobble—had also invited another married woman to his room.

The gals got their timetables mixed. They met—in the hotel corridor outside the vice president's door—one coming out after an hour's session on his bed; the other going in, anticipating her own hour's session.

What followed made Mason City history: a hair-pulling tussle fit for television.

Eventually, somebody found Ralph and sent him scurrying to his room.

He found Marilyn—not in contrite tears, but her Irish temper sky-high. She was furious enough to blurt out insults against the vice president, the other woman—and Ralph Samuelson.

One word led to 20 more. Ralph, usually mild, but adamantly stubborn once he felt somebody had done him wrong, pieced things together.

He discovered that this vice president and Marilyn might have been carrying on an affair for some time.

Ralph terminated his convention business fast. He and Marilyn drove home in the big Continental, through the Iowa cornfields, through the Minnesota hayfields, to the Mazeppa turkey farm, without speaking.

The next day Ralph met one of his friends, Martin Stoddard, a neighbor. Ralph told him what had happened at Mason City. Martin, tall, handsome, well groomed, looked sheepish.

"So it finally came out," he said.

"Finally?"

"Ralph, I hate to tell you this, but since you know some of it, you might as well know it all."

"Know what all?"

"About Marilyn."

"What about Marilyn? She made a mistake, a bad mistake. Got herself involved with a skunk. He seduced her, the swine. I should have knocked his block off. He seduced her, I tell you."

"Ralph," said Martin, trying nervously to light his pipe. "It's—I mean, he wasn't the only one."

That night, after some threats, Marilyn confessed the whole sordid mess.

"I was stunned, sick to my stomach. I had nightmares, couldn't sleep, became a nervous wreck," Ralph tried to describe his feelings years later. "I asked her why this had happened. What had I done to deserve it? Marilyn couldn't think of any reason other than that it had become a game she played and, as she admitted now, finally lost.

"As so many other human beings who get shoved into corners they think they can't get out of, I was ready to kill myself.

"Then, one night—out under the sky, in the familiar spot where I had stared up into the heavens so many times, wondering about God—I broke down, cried like a child.

"I cried out to God to help me through this horrible, tragic defeat. And it seemed, the more I prayed, the more I felt comforted. Somehow, I knew God had heard me, and was giving me strength.

"I didn't realize until later, when Marilyn told me, that I had prayed so loud in the still night, she had heard every word on the porch; and it made her realize, more than before, what she had done to me."

Ralph asked for a divorce. Marilyn didn't contest it, left and went to work in the Twin Cities.

Ralph's divorce became final on December 9, 1947.

{6}

Section

32. HAZEL

Ralph Samuelson had waded through a trough of scalding acid—had experienced bitterness, hatred, self-accusation, shame, humiliation; had played the role of cuckold—and survived.

When he needed him most he found a friend, a young minister, the Reverend Elverado Cox, new pastor at the Mazeppa church.

Ralph confided in him. The pastor offered to pray with him whenever Ralph desired it.

"And very soon, somewhat to my surprise, I was praying that I would be guided to a good wife whom I could trust, one who would give me children, as I did not want to grow old without having a family," Ralph in simple unadorned terms summarized his post-divorce period.

And miraculously—so he described it—in a few weeks he was actually courting blond, beautiful, taken-by-surprise, independent Hazel Thorpe, who had no idea what was going through the mind of her, as yet unknown, suitor.

This time, his courting was different. Said he, "If you have adopted the Lord's way, you will find that when there is a broken heart to deal with, He will work very rapidly to heal it. He knows how."

It began on Thursday, Christmas Day, only 16 days after Ralph's divorce from Marilyn had gone through.

Ralph had difficulty in getting his turkeys fed in time for the 9 o'clock Christmas service at the Mazeppa church, so he decided, that cold, crisp Christmas morning, to drive over and attend the Pine Island church, some nine miles away, also served by the Rev. Cox, his preacher friend. There it happened.

"I sat there listening to the sermon, all about the joy of Christmas and the Child, when suddenly a voice within me spoke very clearly, 'There is your wife.'

"As if by magic, my eyes were drawn over to the extreme right side of the church, where sat a radiantly blond, ravishingly beautiful young woman. I had never seen her before.

"As I found out later, she just happened to be visiting a girl friend who lived in Pine Island. She was a teacher in Austin, the big meatpacking city, some 70 miles south.

"I said to myself, how can this be since we've never even been introduced? But I knew that God would take care of that little matter, too, as He can do anything, if only we put our trust in Him. So I decided to wait and let the Lord get us properly introduced."

Apparently, the good Lord took time out to take care of that little chore, even before the old year was up, on New Year's Eve.

Ralph got misty-eyed when he talked about it. Those were the days when devout church members didn't go to a hotel or a tavern on New Year's Eve to dance, get drunk, shout a bibulous "Happeee New Year," and kiss other men's wives. They went to church, prayed the old year out, the new one in!

The little wooden Methodist church at Pine Island, almost as wide as it is long, was filled. When Ralph came in, only one seat was still vacant, in the rear pew. He sat down.

Ralph doesn't know how to explain it, but he found himself sitting right next to the blond girl!

The preacher's wife was there, too.

And, thus, Hazel Thorpe and Ralph Samuelson were properly introduced in the first exciting minutes of 1948.

"I was almost speechless, I was so thrilled," Ralph remembered. "I didn't want to be stupid and frighten her away, so I went home and thought the matter over.

"I decided it was time for me to act, as I couldn't expect the good Lord to do everything for me," said Ralph, with a straight face. "I knew I still remembered how to court a young lady, as I had plenty practice in my younger days."

And court her he did. First he called her, made a date to take her to the Anchor Inn, an "All You Can Eat" chicken, ham, fish, and shrimp emporium of the area. Ralph didn't seem to remember what they ate. But he remembered taking the beautiful Hazel home, all the way back to Austin, in his willow-green Lincoln Continental, one of those early 12-cylinder jobs, so she wouldn't have to take the bus back. He let her drive part of the way and got up courage enough to clear the decks for honest action in the future by telling her frankly about his divorce. But he did not tell her the good Lord had given him definite assurance that he was going to marry Hazel Thorpe.

He made further dates, drove Hazel to Hopkins, just west of the Twin Cities to let her visit her foster-sister and brother-in-law, who cultivated a raspberry farm—a place Ralph was never to forget.

Spring came; the sap ran. Ralph's ardor grew.

He came to a conclusion: Since the Lord had promised Hazel to him anyway, why wait?

So, one Sunday evening, while driving home on winding U.S. 12 from Janesville, Wisconsin, Ralph asked Hazel to marry him.

She didn't commit herself, said she'd have to postpone any decision until her teaching contract ran out in June.

Ralph couldn't wait that long, begged her to get a release. Hazel talked to her principal. Apparently God was still on Ralph's side, for the school official agreed to look for a replacement. He found one—in two weeks—and gave Hazel her release.

Minnesota had a six-month waiting period after a divorce, so the couple, she 30, he 45, decided to cross the border to Decorah, Iowa, to get married.

They did, at the Methodist church, on April 10, 1948.

"The time of the wedding was 2 p.m., our pastor was the Reverend Elverado Cox, Ralph's friend and mine," said Hazel, who had her own memories of this wedding and the whirlwind courtship which preceded it.

"Some people complained that it was too windy, and chilly. But to me it was a glorious, sunny day—all signs of nature pointing to a fresh beginning, new life. And so it was with me," said Hazel, her brilliantly blue eyes glistening a little with memories. "I was on the beautiful threshold of a new life. I'm sure I'd have felt the same if it had been snowing and the drifts had been five feet high.

"Only a few close relations and intimate friends were invited. The church (I've never been back there) I remember for the stability it represented, for it was built of brick, looked sturdy. The interior had richly polished wood.

"My feelings? What a mixture of emotions! I'd been near the altar on several occasions, but I loved my independence and my career more than the man of the moment. I could always find more reasons not to marry than to do so.

"For one thing, I was the product of a broken home, which undoubtedly made me very cautious. And let me be honest, I was having a pretty good time by myself in my own style. I wasn't in the least concerned about my unwedded state, as so many of my friends.

"Then, during those eventful Christmas holidays of 1947-48, I met Ralph. He was an entirely new experience for me. He was older, very persistent and persuasive—always a perfect gentleman. He put me on such a high pedestal, that I found myself being a better person—just so I wouldn't let him down.

"The power of positive thinking must have swept me off my feet, for I found myself, somewhat astonished, in Decorah, saying 'I do!'

"I suppose I was so impressed by Ralph's courtliness, his sincerity, and his avowed claim that he would be devastated if I didn't accept him, that I did accept him. No one had ever seemed to need me so much or had made me feel such a desirable woman."

33. THE NEW LIFE

After a short honeymoon at the swank, luxurious Nicolett Hotel in Minneapolis, it was back to the farm, for it was turkey hatching season.

It was the same farm, the same turkey buildings, the same house, but a different Ralph. And a different life.

Hazel was now part of it.

First she fixed up the house.

And she made noble, successful efforts to learn the complicated turkey business. For an instructor of English, that was quite a switch.

Ralph was a good teacher, she a willing pupil. Soon the two made a good team, even branding their own pedigreed stock, loading poults on the station wagon, which had special heaters and fans to keep the chicks warm during trips to farms sometimes several hundred miles away.

Hazel was an excellent cook, never afraid to try new recipes or perfect old ones. And Ralph liked everything she made.

She induced him to join her church, and together they adopted the system of tithing, giving one-tenth of all their profits to the church.

One worry Ralph should have had, Hazel's doctor had told her she couldn't have any children.

Ralph Samuelson reacted with typical assurance, "Baloney. I can't accept that because the Lord has promised me children."

So sure was he that he'd have these children, in spite of the diagnosis of the best doctors, that he planned to dispose of his small, two-bedroom house and build a larger one—with room for offspring, on the same spot where the old one had stood. The discarded house would be rolled away to stand on a corner in Mazeppa.

With indomitable optimism, Ralph went through the whole routine—sketches, architect's drawings, estimates, blueprints of a building 100 feet long, with a 24-foot double garage.

The dream house would be partly of expensive, gray-brown Kasota stone and marble. It would have a 30-foot living room, two complete bathrooms, three fireplaces in various parts of the house to supplement the baseboard heating, a seven-foot stone chimney with four flues, huge thermo glass picture windows, folding doors everywhere, dishwasher in the kitchen, gigantic refrigerator, completely equipped laundry room, a spacious porch with tall white colonial pillars—the whole topped off with a decorative weathervane atop a deluxe cupola.

Ralph worked long hours with the architect, hired a crew of workers who went to work with a will, began construction of a building which eventually was to cost more than twice as much as the original estimate.

It was to grow into one of Ralph Samuelson's bigger and unending worries!

34. SKIS REDISCOVERED

Lake City, on the shore of Ralph's Lake Pepin, had been touched by the years—not dramatically, but slowly, persistently, progressively.

New buildings had gone up, old storefronts were renovated, streets improved; schools grew, were consolidated, a new addition to the high school was voted; a new flour mill was built; new parks opened, new churches were dedicated, new supermarkets came to town. But the greatest change, physically, materialized in the marina area, that part of the lakefront Ralph Samuelson knew so well—where he had grown up.

One by one, the old buildings lining the harbor were coming down—the button factory, the old power house where Ralph used to make some of his repairs, the junk yard, the Botsford Lumber Yard where he got his wood for his skis, shacks used by the fishermen, including Walt Anderson's.

Back in the days when Ben Simons watched his hero do the impossible, the harbor had one small opening, cut through the north bank of the pond where Ralph and his friends swam in the nude.

In 1933, a project had been completed deepening the north outlet, reinforcing it with vertical walls and pilings. The entire land area of the 12-acre point was raised several feet to overcome frequent flooding.

Then in 1946, this exit was closed entirely, and an opening made on the southeast side to keep out the ice in winter.

All this time, the Lake City Waterfront Commission, chaired by Lake City's respected publisher, Larry Oberg, and the City Council were being pestered by a young man who was apparently dedicating his whole life to a dream—providing a modern harbor where yachts and runabouts, motorboats, cruisers, sailboats and rowboats from up and down the mighty river could dock in comfort and safety.

Some far-sighted citizens did what they could to go one step farther, attempt to get a modern motel located on that historic point which had witnessed the beginning of water skiing.

Feasibility reports were prepared by professionals, at considerable cost; numerous big motel chains were approached. None was interested enough to pursue the matter of building a fine tourist motel on what many, even today, consider the most desirable and picturesque point of land along the Mississippi from St. Louis to St. Paul.

When progress in that direction slowed, Ben Simons, now in his maturing years, pursued his dream all the more energetically.

He believed Lake City's new harbor could be financed with government money, if the proper authorities were approached. Eventually, the national government actually did allocate half a million dollars for a harbor and marina enlargement project, much of it on property purchased with admissions collected at Ralphs' water ski shows.

Meanwhile, the annual waterfront shows went on without Ralph. Water carnivals they were called now; Ben Simons was committee chairman.

The events got bigger and better, with contests for Fete Queens, swimming competitions across Lake Pepin, boat races, ski demonstrations, concessions, professional announcers, loud speakers, and policing by the Coast Guard.

Apparently nobody thought of inviting Ralph Samuelson. People didn't even know what had become of him.

A grand climax—also an anti-climax, as it turned out—came in 1948, the same year in which Hazel and Ralph took up their love life in the old house, soon to make room for Ralph's dream house.

Ben Simons was again the chairman. The carnival was combined with the Fourth of July events; the Louis R. McCahill Legion Post was the sponsor. The Lake City American Legion Post, which later helped to promote Samuelson, was named after Louis McCahill, who died in World War I. Alice McCahill, widow of James McCahill, Louis's brother, was the last McCahill to live in

Lake City, before she moved to Charlottesville, Virginia.

Ben began to make plans months ahead—for speedboat demonstrations, girl ballet swimmers, a parachute leap with a veteran of military jumps bailing out at low altitude, diving exhibitions, the usual three-mile swim across the lake, an appearance by the reigning Minneapolis Aquatennial Queen, Patty McLane, fireworks with Clellan Card of WCCO radio fame as master of ceremonies, band music, and puppets for the kids.

As a very special attraction, the famous water skiing Aquabats of Cypress Gardens, Florida, who would perform precision tricks and acrobatic stunts, even do a complete ski somersault from the jump ramp. At night, the team of two men and a girl would put on an amazing nocturnal show, using torches and colored flares.

Water skiing had come a long way since it was invented on that same Lake in 1922.

Whether it was all this emphasis on skiing or not, Ben Simons didn't recall. But he suddenly had an idea, to show how much progress had actually been made in the sport. He remembered when as self-styled little punk he had seen Ralph Samuelson do his very first stunt on water skis.

He wondered—where was Samuelson? Were his old boards still in existence somewhere? Wouldn't it be something if he could find them, put them on display at this, the best water carnival he had ever put on?

It took some research, but eventually he found out that Ralph Samuelson was a turkey farmer somewhere near Mazeppa or Zumbro Falls or Zumbrota.

He hadn't seen much of him since he got married to that Irish girl, what was her name? He'd been divorced; Ben had heard.

The telephone operator helped him out. Ben got Ralph's number, called him and asked if he could see him.

"Be happy to meet you again," Ralph told him. "What's it about?"

"Tell you when I see you."

Ben drove his old truck to Ralph's farm and was introduced to Ralph's new bride. They had coffee, chatted. Then Ben, one of the most modest of men, came out with it, "Ralph, you still have those old skis—you know, the ones you used for your first skiing?"

"The first ones, no. One broke, remember?"

"I had forgotten that," admitted Ben.

"But I made exact duplicates, you recall. Improved them a bit. I did my jumping and speed skiing on them. Why?"

"I'd like to put them on display for our water carnival."

"Display? Those old boards?"

"To show how different modern skis are. You still got 'em?"

"I guess so. Somewhere out in the barn, up in the rafters somewhere..."

Hazel interrupted. "What in the world is all this about?"

Ralph explained, sketchily. He had never told Hazel much about his water skiing. It seemed too long ago

"Could we look for them?" asked Ben.

"Sure. Let's go."

"If you let me borrow them, I'll take good care of them," promised Ben.

"Sure, why not," said Ralph. "My water ski days are over. These skis really belong to Lake City and Lake Pepin. Never realized how much I've missed that Lake."

They found the old relics, up in the highest rafters, covered with layers of dust, pigeon droppings, mouse kernels. But they were intact, solid as ever, and sound.

Carefully, they cleaned them a bit.

With visions of how fine the skis would look in Lake City, Ben put them carefully into the back of his truck.

Hazel was staring in silence. She had never seen two more weird-looking skis.

Ralph had another idea. He went into the house, opened an

old drawer, found some of the pictures Grace Eaton had taken. He gave Ben a few.

Back in Lake City, Ben Simons put the skis and the pictures on display in the most conspicious show window in town—the Collins Drugstore, corner of Lyons and Lakeshore Drive.

There they remained during the carnival—and for some weeks afterward. People stared at them, shook their heads in wonder.

The big water show came off as planned.

But there was an aftermath; the carnival was a financial bust.

Said Ben Simons, almost as laconically as Ralph would have done, "In 1948 the water carnival lost $10,000, and after it was over, everything was stored up in the attic of my Ben Franklin Building on Center Street."

That meant that the skis, which had been gathering dust in Ralph's barn, would now be gathering city dust instead of country dust in the cluttered upper rooms of a store.

They gathered dust for five full years before anybody ever saw them again.

35. THE TUMOR

Whether Ralph's incurable faith had anything to do with it or not no doctor will admit, but only a year after they were married, Hazel became extremely worried.

She was developing a tumor in her stomach—growing perceptibly.

Ralph, also worried sick, insisted she go to a specialist at the Mayo Clinic, Rochester.

Hazel went. The examination was remarkably short.

"You have a tumor, all right," the doctor informed Hazel. "Of course, we can't be sure yet whether it's a boy or a girl."

When Hazel told him, Ralph was thunderstruck, elated, but wondering how it could have happened,

"Must I explain it?" asked Hazel. "You did it—you and that unshakable faith of yours!"

Karen was born on October 14, 1949, before the new house was finished. But Baby Karen had respiratory trouble. The doctor was very discouraging, since he and his wife had lost their own baby recently from the same cause.

"I spent a lot of time praying for this little girl," Ralph recalled.

Eventually, the X-rays showed improvement. Karen's lungs were clearing up!

Ralph simply called it another miracle to add to his growing list.

While the final touches were put on the new house, and after the old one had been moved away on huge rollers, Hazel and Karen moved into the hatchery, which Hazel fixed up into livable quarters.

When the new house was finally ready, came the task of buying furniture.

"We went on a buying spree," remembered Ralph, "and purchased a new electric stove and refrigerator and dishwasher. Our doors and trim around the windows were of blond birch, so we selected blond furniture. It was beautiful."

"I had saved about $500 from my teaching salary, and I blew that, too," Hazel admitted.

But unseen trouble was just beyond the horizon, first created incongruously enough by the beautiful new house.

When Ralph realized that it had cost him twice as much as he had anticipated, or as the architect had indicated, he had to borrow money from his sister-in-law—the one on the raspberry farm—to help pay part of the bills that had piled up.

The sister-in-law was a realistic bargainer. She demanded a mortgage on the farm and the buildings as security.

Ralph wasn't worried. He'd pay everything off when that year's turkeys were marketed.

He couldn't anticipate, as he read his Bible in the evenings, that very soon he'd be like one of its most dramatic and unenviable characters, Job. He couldn't imagine that he would soon have more agonies than that classic example of personified tribulation.

36. CHOLERA

One day in that unforgettable summer of 1950, Ralph and Hazel noticed some of their turkeys looked a little droopy.

The next morning they discovered five carcasses out in the open field.

Ralph, as always convinced there was purpose in everything, that God tested those He loved but never tested them beyond their endurance, rushed several of the dead birds to the University of Minnesota farm near the Twin Cities.

The verdict he was given by the medical examiners would have shattered the strongest heart.

Ralph's turkeys had cholera!

By the time the diagnosis was made, it was already too late. The disease was spreading with deadly speed among Ralph's 15,000 birds.

In spite of special medication prescribed by the best university experts, turkeys died—by the dozen, by the score, by the hundreds, by the thousands, until 10,000, two-thirds of the entire flock, lay buried in mass graves.

Eventually the flock was decimated—and still going down.

But expenses kept going up. The three farms, a total of over 500 acres, required hired help that had to be paid. The medicine for the sick birds was expensive; special diets were exorbitantly dear.

Ralph prayed. It helped, Ralph insisted later. If God had not been at his elbow constantly, he would have lost his mind.

He managed to save just enough of his breeding flock so he could start over again the next spring.

But the profits for the year, and the year after that, were shot. The money that did come in had to be used to pay off the worst debts.

In spite of the weight on his sore back—which bothered him still so much that he never had a single night without pain—Ralph kept going.

He put his brooder hens—beautiful, softly clucking birds, although they panicked just as quickly as all turkeys—into isolation. He kept them calm enough so they'd lay eggs, which went into the modern, new incubators. Ralph planned to sell day-old poults to turkey growers who wanted birds for early market.

He thought he had many waiting customers. Turkey growers everywhere knew about him. Before his trouble with the cholera, he had made an enviable name for himself, had even been honored—not as the inventor of water skiing, which nobody remembered, but as a turkey pioneer.

One of the biggest recognitions that can come to turkey farmers, the equivalent of an Oscar or an Emmy, had come to him. He was featured on the front cover of the official publication of the Minnesota Turkey Growers Association, the *Minnesota Gobbles*, in the December 1949 edition.

The front cover shows the vast estate of Ralph Samuelson, his beautiful rambler house, with the fancy chimney, the brooder houses, the incubator sheds, the barns—all lying in that peaceful Minnesota Valley like a rich man's dream fulfilled.

The lower half of the cover carries another picture, Ralph, his hair still combed back and parted in the middle, his Long Swedish profile wearing a half-smile, his right hand in his pocket, the other holding open the metal door of a Jamesway incubator, showing 15 trays of turkey eggs.

Says the article, in part:

> The cover of the December issue of "Minnesota Gobbles" features the Samuelson Turkey Ranch and Hatchery of Mazeppa, as it appears today. This is a far cry from its appearance when Samuelson entered the turkey field, some 17 years ago.
>
> At the time of his commencement in the business of growing

turkeys little was known of their habits, scientific breeding, disease and the many other problems facing him as well as hundreds of others about the state making this venture.

During these days disease was their biggest problem. Death loss from disease reaching 50 percent was a common occurrence. Today, disease is controlled by sanitary methods that have been tried over and over again and proven successful. In Minnesota the reduction and eradication of many of the disease problems for growers can be credited to such scientists as Dr. W.A. Billings, Dr. Benj. S. Pomeroy, and to Dr. H.R. Sloan, all of the University Farm staff ...

The Samuelson Turkey Ranch and Hatchery have grown from a start of but 47 acres of land and a small 50 egg sized incubator. Today three farms comprising over 500 acres of land, and a most modern battery of incubators, are used to carry on his operations. In the industry, Mr. Samuelson has expressed an opinion that the Turkey Industry is crossing the threshold of a new era that will see turkey on the tables of the nation, the year 'round, and in keen competition with pork and beef.

The large farm is pictured on top with Mr. Samuelson and his battery of incubators below.

Ralph must have groaned miserably when he read again about the conquered diseases after his turkeys had died from sickness that was supposed to have been controlled, according to the article.

Then came worse. Ralph discovered he couldn't even sell his poults; couldn't find buyers; even received cancellations of orders already confirmed. Everybody was suddenly afraid of buying turkeys from a place where cholera had struck!

But there was more trouble in the wings of Ralph's theatre of woe.

He had been not only a turkey farmer, but a grain and cattle man, with 350 acres under cultivation in grain for his turkeys—and for some unusual cattle he had purchased on impulse: a registered, purebred Hereford bull, and four heifers, beautiful, dark-red animals with white faces.

"We had hoped to start a herd of this kind, as I had always

liked to look at them, and they go real good in the freezer," Ralph explained with naive oversimplification. He had paid $450 each for these animals when they were still calves.

The bull had done his eager work on all four willing heifers, and it was time for their calves to arrive.

Another blow. Something else went wrong.

When the heifers were in labor, it was discovered that the calves of all of them were too large for normal births, nobody knew why. The only vet available had no solution. Nobody did.

The desperate and crude emergency method of using a block and tackle to promote births killed the calves, and injured the beautiful heifers so they could never walk again. They had to be slaughtered.

Even the meat was badly damaged from internal bleeding.

The whole herd was a total loss, except the bull. Ralph sold him for a mere $500.

"Talk about a nightmare!" remembered Ralph. "I couldn't sleep for a week. I wondered how I could ever have so much trouble."

Then he added with typical Swedish understatement: "My child-like faith was sure being tested."

So it was. But somehow he worked himself out of this valley too.

"I had to ask God daily for strength and faith to accept this terrible blow. I knew, somehow, that the good Lord was testing my faith under fire. He sure was zeroing in on me.

"But I made up my mind, no matter what happened, I'd trust Him. I tried to make like Job who said, 'Though He slay me, yet will I trust in Him.'

"But I sure wondered, often and long, how this cruel destruction could turn to good. Common sense told me that nothing good could possibly come from torturing my poor Herefords, killing my helpless, innocent turkeys.

"For little did I dream then, an ordinary farmer, who had never gone beyond the eighth grade, who had done what none had succeeded in doing—skied on water—but who had been completely and thoroughly forgotten, that I would someday gain enough attention so people would actually listen to me.

"And I might as well admit it. Telling about these failures of mine, these hard knocks—and there are more to come, alas—takes greater courage and faith than I had the day I first skied on Lake Pepin.

"But out there on my Lake I sure wasn't giving God any credit. I was an eternity away from Him.

"Things had gone well with *me*. I was giving myself all the credit.

"But that night, out under the stars, all that changed. I knew God was somewhere—within reach, even of me.

"He wanted me to realize one thing—that we need God. Some of us won't realize that until we have so much trouble that we have no other place to go but to Him."

37. ERYSIPELAS

"Anticipating a second child, when originally we were told we couldn't even have one, should have been a deliriously happy event," Ralph philosophized later. "But with all the trouble we were having, we did not exactly look forward to it."

Both Hazel and Ralph worried. Where would the money come from to keep up the business? And having babies had changed, too. They were no longer delivered for $2.50.

Babies care little, it seems, about the trouble ahead when their time comes. Deborah Jane was born on a cold—30 below zero—Minnesota day, January 24, 1951. They brought her home, put her crib close to one of the expensive fireplaces, blazing to keep her warm.

Ralph, meanwhile, was trying desperately to start a new flock. He made some progress, but the bank account was so low, he had no working capital at all.

Then, a persistent creditor threatened a lawsuit if he didn't get paid the $1,200 Ralph owed him. Deadline, three days.

Ralph called on his friend, the minister.

"We will ask God for help," said the Reverend Cox.

"But will He help?" asked Ralph. "I only have three days."

"Do you believe He will?"

"I want to believe."

"That's not enough, Ralph. You must believe He will."

"I know He can. If He wants to.

"He won't, as long as you have doubt. Shall we pray your doubts away?"

"Please!" pleaded Ralph.

They did. At the end of the session, Ralph rose from his knees, exclaiming, "Reverend Cox, while we were praying, I had a clear image of a certain man in Rochester. I've done business with him. I could hear God telling me to go and see him."

"Then do as God asks," said the Reverend Cox.

Ralph went to Rochester, found his man, told him about his need. Ralph stated the result laconically.

"The man simply opened a drawer of his desk, pulled out an envelope with exactly $1,200 in bills, and said, 'This is between you and me and God. This is your money now, not to be repaid. It is my tithe, and I was saving it for God's use. He sent you to me. Take it.'"

Ralph did and got his creditor off his back.

"We had been hit by cholera, but we had saved enough birds to start again; hope was beginning to sprout in our hearts. By fall, we actually had 10,000 beautiful, big bronze turkeys on a new piece of land I hadn't used before. Being new ground was important, for it would be free of all disease germs, or so we thought ... in our ignorance."

Ralph's birds were almost large enough for market—12-14 pounds for the hens, and 20-25 pounds for the toms. They would bring at least $10 each, totaling $100,000.

Of course, that wasn't all clear. Ralph had a feed bill of about

$40,000 tied up in those birds, all the money he could borrow.

But that would leave at least $50,000—enough to pay all other debts.

Then, tragedy pounced again—like a scourge!

This time it was the dread erysipelas, caused by a streptococcus germ, bringing with it fever, weakness, death.

Ralph and Hazel were never to forget that ugly-sounding name.

The disease spread even faster than the cholera. It rampaged through the dressing pens, through the brooder houses, through the flocks on the open range.

The turkeys' heads turned bright red with high fever and swelled up, and the birds dropped over, never to get to their powerful legs again.

So many died so fast, Ralph and his hired man had to bury the carcasses with two tractors, scooping out a whole hillside, then covering the valuable birds with dirt.

For years afterward, Ralph couldn't drive down Minnesota Highway 60, the old Indian trail from Zumbrota to Zumbro Falls, without turning his face away when he passed that particular hillside where God had tested him almost beyond his endurance.

"We buried the turkeys steadily until there were none left," said Ralph, with more Swedish understatement. "None."

It was the biggest loss of his life.

Back in 1939, when a sneak blizzard had crept up on Minnesota farmers and hunters on Armistice Day, November 11—with the temperature going down from a pleasant 50 in the forenoon to 10 below zero with heavy snows in eight hours—Ralph had lost about $10,000 in frozen turkeys. He hadn't even complained about that.

His loss in 1950, from the cholera, had been $50,000.

This time it was over $100,000.

That fall, there was no income. That winter, Ralph tried stubbornly to start a new flock. He succeeded partly; but, once again, nobody would buy his poults come spring, because of the usual fear of disease carry-over. So Ralph had no working capital to feed a new flock. And his credit was gone.

Hazel, especially, was worried. Her third baby was on the way.

John Thomas, known as Jon, waited until August 23, 1952, before he made his appearance.

Somehow Ralph found the money for the hospital expenses.

But the big one was turning into a veritable nightmare—that $40,000 feed bill.

God's little miracles kept on happening, of course. At one time, when another creditor was threatening to put the law on him at once, Ralph opened his mail, hesitantly, for it had become ugly with demands for payments of bills, threats of legal action, nasty personal letters. But this morning, there it was—a check for $1,000.

Not from Heaven—not directly—although Ralph insisted it came from there somehow.

For years, he had sold turkeys to a farmer's cooperative elevator. That co-op had terminated its business and was paying off its members. Ralph was one.

He paid off his tormentor, but it was just a stopgap.

Several of Ralph's creditors got together, threatened him, until the pressure on him was simply too great.

On the advice of a lawyer, Ralph Samuelson—the man who invented water skiing, something that would make him a millionaire if it happened today; the father of three young children; the man who once was rich—had to declare bankruptcy.

And in the Middle West that is as close to a disgrace as disgrace gets.

38. BANKRUPTCY

It was a painful time, full of humiliation, mental anguish, legal hassles, lawyers, court decisions, bank clerks, fees, scorching letters, abject apologies, loss of friends, ridicule—all the misery of bankruptcy proceedings.

On top of it all, Ralph had to return to Lake City for another sad family event—the funeral of his father.

Charles, age 83, had outlived his wife, Mary, by 20 years.

"Father was never the same after mother died," Ralph said.

"But father lived long enough to see all his grandchildren and came often to our turkey ranch at Mazeppa to visit us—before we had all our trouble. He helped with the chores and at corn husking time.

"He was a very kind father, and I loved him very much, as I did my mother. I can't remember ever being punished by him. He was kind to children, especially to his grandchildren, of course. He loved animals, and before he became crippled with arthritis and moved to live with my sister, Harriet, in St. Peter. He was known for his way with the squirrels around Lake Pepin. They climbed all over him to get the nuts he always carried for them. He is at rest now, with mother and the boys who went before them."

After the funeral, the usual busy tongues wagged in Lake City. The news of Samuelson's failure preceded him. Some merchants had lost money when Ralph declared bankruptcy.

Ralph Samuelson didn't feel so big now in the town's eyes, or in his own.

He was compelled to announce a sale of all his farm machinery and turkey equipment to pay off as many debts as he could. All he had left was a set of empty buildings. And the future looked empty too.

Dan Bren, Hazel's brother-in-law, loved the Samuelson children as if they were his own.

But Ralph's mortgage on his farm and buildings was held by Dan's wife, Hazel's foster-sister.

She was beginning to hint darkly about foreclosure. She eyed the turkey farm, without turkeys or cattle. And even without Ralph, who was trying to earn a few dollars plowing for his neighbor, Howard Badensick. That helped just enough to get money for groceries.

"I wasn't sure what the good Lord had in mind, or what he was going to do next," Ralph summed up.

Ralph didn't even have money to pay his light bill. His electricity was cut off. Unable to even cook a hot meal, Hazel did the sensible thing. She took the children and went up to her sister's place at Hopkins, the raspberry farm.

Ralph was incurably optimistic even then. "I had been in many circumstances like this before, so I told the good Lord that I needed help soon, or I'd lose my wife and children.

"I guess it was about then I read something I've never forgotten, 'When you come to the end of your rope, tie a knot in it, and hang on!' I did just that."

One answer came from a neighbor, Laverne Windhorst, a quiet, soft-spoken man, who asked if he could rent some of the land, even advanced $400 in cash.

Ralph paid his electric bill.

But by now Ralph had an additional handicap. He had wrenched his back again—aggravating his old ailment. The doctor ordered him to go to bed at once.

Lying there alone, unable to get up, depending on neighbors to come and feed him, Ralph Samuelson had reached another deep, personal valley.

"Just as I was beginning to feel so sorry for myself, I didn't want to live, when I was on the very verge of losing my faith in God, a man called on me. He was the answer to my prayers."

The man was Edward Simmons of Altura, a small town near Winona, an old river town on the Mississippi. Simmons was manager of a large feed mill, a turkey dressing plant, and turkey hatchery. Ralph had done business with him.

Ed had a problem.

"He had a problem! He wanted me to help him," remembered

Ralph, still incredulous. "What a switch."

Ed had thousands of young turkeys about six weeks old, and not enough room for them. Within an hour Ralph and Ed had made a deal. Ed was willing to furnish used equipment, a used Ford truck, pay $50 a week in cash to keep Ralph going; Ralph, in turn, would take care of the young birds, later let them range on his farm.

"In one day I was out of bed, ready to go to work."

Ed sent thousands of young turkeys to Ralph's farm—equipment, even feed and men to help fill the feeders and waterers.

Within a few weeks Ralph was actually back in business. First he called Hazel to give her the good tidings. Hazel and the three children hurried back at once, happy—more than happy.

The happiness of that reunion Ralph never forgot. He was soon to need pleasant memories.

39. THE SKIS AGAIN

Had Ralph been less sad and harassed when he attended his father's funeral in Lake City, he might have met two old friends … his skis.

While Ralph had all his trouble with turkeys, Ben Simons hadn't been idle. True, the 1948 carnival had lost money, but Ben was fundamentally optimistic.

For one thing, he insisted the city should have a new bathhouse to replace the old one, which wasn't worthy to be called a shed, much less a house.

Ben wanted a place with cabins for swimmers to change, a concession stand, an office; he wanted lifeguards, a new diving tower, a better diving platform.

Finally the city, after many board meetings and some heated discussions by the city council and the Waterfront Board, agreed to finance such a bathhouse—clean, modern, with showers, a loud-speaker system to page parents.

It was while equipping and decorating the modest but efficient brick building that Ben Simons once again remembered Ralph's old skis.

He had to think. Where were they anyway? They had last been on display at the 1948 carnival. Ah, yes. He had put them in storage. Where? Of course. In his own storage room on top of the Ben Franklin Store, on West Center.

This time he wouldn't even have to ask anybody for permission, since obviously Ralph didn't worry about those old boards.

Ben decided to get them, use them for decoration, to spruce up the marine atmosphere of the new bathhouse.

Besides, it would lend a sense of history to the place.

And history there was all around that bathhouse. Every time Ben looked at the growing, improving waterfront, he encountered history.

He wondered, did Samuelson have the faintest idea what he started with those old skis Ben was going to put on public display once again?

He retrieved the two antique skis, blew the dust of five years off them, took them to the new bathhouse, and carefully attached them to the south wall, next to the candy counter. He found the old pictures Ralph had given him, got a few more from Grace Eaton's sister, Mabel, Mrs. Morgan Mabin. He also found an old newspaper clipping somebody had saved.

Above the skis he tacked a homemade placard with antique lettering:

WORLD'S FIRST WATER SKIS

Ben wasn't absolutely sure if they actually were the world's first water skis; but it wasn't too likely that anybody would, or could, go to the trouble of proving they were not.

So there they hung.

A few visitors did look at those queer old boards. But most of them didn't really give a damn—or didn't believe the caption.

How could these be the world's first water skis?

There probably had been water skis as long as there had been water, said some of the young Lake Pepin skiers, skimming along on shorter, narrower, better molded, much more efficient skis, behind fast boats, enjoying the exhilarating sport, paying less than no heed to the thought that perhaps somebody, somewhere, sometime had actually used those monsters for the first time.

Even Ralph Samuelson didn't know they were there.

"I didn't get to Lake City often," Ralph remembered later. "I didn't see those skis for 10 more years. Anyway, so much had happened since I was on them!

"Once upon a time, my Lake and I had lived on intimate terms, and she had let me ski on her with those dear old boards on my feet. But now all that was just another dream."

Ralph had had several of them, and some had turned into nightmares.

Another nightmare was coming up.

40. PARATYPHOID

Whether it was wise for Ralph to branch out again in the turkey business, he wasn't sure later. But two years after working successfully with his partner, Ed Simmons, he did just that.

A certain Frank Kramer from Red Wing contacted Ralph. He owned a turkey ranch on the plateau overlooking Old Frontenac, historic village famous as the site of the first fort on the Minnesota shore of Lake Pepin—Fort Beauharnois. One of its French officers is supposed to have named Pepin after a cousin in France.

The ranch was on a spot not unknown to Ralph—the identical place where he had learned to fly in his affluent years.

The airport, too, had gone bankrupt, like Ralph. Not a good omen. But the hangar shed, about 200 feet long and 100 wide, was solid. It had been converted into a turkey roost, with slat floors. Part of it was made into a rearing porch, 1,000 feet long, big enough to hold about 20,000 broilers, birds six weeks old.

Ralph bought the place on a contract for a deed, for nearly $50,000. Annual payments were to be $5,000.

In addition to the sheds, the place included 125 acres of cropland, which Ralph immediately put into soybeans. The first crop was good. Ralph had no difficulty making his first payment.

Joy was back. Success was around, the corner—every corner.

For two years more, Ralph operated both farms. Things were looking up for everybody.

Ralph felt he had finally reached another plateau, a quiet one of happiness and security. Bitter memories of the bankruptcy lingered. They were painfully revived when he met creditors who had lost money on him. But it was wonderful to be with the kids, buy them things, play with them, tease them, watch them grow and learn.

Life was good!

Then, as if the Devil himself were riding on Ralph Samuelson's still sore back, more bad luck came sneaking in the front door of the beautiful house in the valleys—rather through every door and window and crevice of the turkey roost.

Ralph Samuelson, with that incredible faith which few can understand, in retrospect stated simply: "The good Lord never intended for me to stay in the turkey business. So Providence changed things for me."

First, Ed Simmons, Ralph's partner in their successful, joint venture, died of a heart attack.

He was succeeded by his young cousin Harry, who took all the profits of the year, impounded them, and put them aside as a cushion in case they had a loss.

Ralph was running a tight payroll; his bank account was never big. He had to object.

There was friction.

There also was tragedy.

Harry wanted to economize. So he bought hatching eggs from a new source, which was offering them at a bargain.

What the seller didn't tell Harry was that the eggs were diseased.

The disease, this time, was paratyphoid, carried in the egg, and transmitted directly to the embryo turkey.

Mortality rate from paratyphoid among turkeys is terrific.

Ralph was taking about 4,000 day-old poults from Harry every two weeks, at 70 cents each, a total bill of nearly $6,000 a month—not to mention the bill for 1,000 tons of feed a year.

Without warning, the baby turkeys just fell over and died.

Ralph's losses ran to 25, 50, 75 percent—and kept going up with each purchase.

Not only did the tragedy strike up at Frontenac; the same thing happened at Mazeppa, since Ralph's breeding stock came from the same eggs.

Ralph finally lost all birds in both places. All!

Again, he had to shut down all operations. He lost the Frontenac farm, on which he had paid $10,000. It went back to its previous owner.

It was 1957. Ralph Samuelson was broke again—at 54.

Not old, but not young; certainly not young enough to find a new job somewhere. Nobody wanted anybody over 50.

Nobody.

41. FORECLOSURE

Ralph doesn't like to talk too much about the next five years, 1957-1962.

Hazel went back to her chosen profession—teaching; got a job at the Pine Island Elementary School.

"I never went back into the turkey business again but continued to get part-time work wherever I could," Ralph explained. "I also took care of the children when Hazel was away teaching. She drove back and forth, nine miles each way, every weekday. I did most of the cooking for the family."

Ralph must have doubted just a little that God was in his corner when word reached him that his friend, Dan Bren—the man who had prevented Hazel's foster-sister from foreclosing on Ralph's mortgage—was dead.

Once he was gone, his widow foreclosed on her foster-sister's husband.

Relenting somewhat, the sister gave permission for the Samuelsons to stay on the farm for one more year.

Then she sold the whole property to Ralph's neighbor, LaVerne Windhorst.

LaVerne, who became a successful pig farmer on the former turkey ranch, stipulated he wouldn't sign the papers until she would buy the Samuelson family a home in Pine Island, the small town of 1,500 where Hazel had been teaching.

She agreed, and bought Ralph a house in town at the cost of $16,000. From a 500-acre farm, to a small yard; from a $50,000 dream mansion to a small, shingle-sided house worth less than a third as much—to most human beings it would have seemed like a bitter, humiliating come-down, a defeat.

To Ralph Samuelson?

42. THE MIRACLE

All this time, Ralph had teen tortured by his compression fracture. The nerves of his spine were pinched. He was unable to move without pain, which at times became excruciating. But when the deadline approached to leave the farm, Ralph insisted on doing some of the clean-up chores.

He was dismantling a building that had collapsed from the heavy snow of the previous winter. The long power wires going to the building had to be removed. So Ralph, crippled as he was, put a ladder against a 20-foot pole, climbed to the top, and proceeded to cut them.

Had he been a professional lineman, he would never have snipped all the wires on one side first. But he did. When he severed the last one, the uncut strands on the other side simply yanked the pole over, snapping it off at the base.

It went crashing down. So did the ladder, with Ralph on it.

He plummeted to the ground, landing on his wrists, his head missing a cement wall by inches.

"As I lay there, my wrists burning, my whole body bruised, I said to God, 'Lord, what are you up to now? What good could come out of a fall like this?'" Ralph remembered.

Ralph managed to crawl out from under the tangle of wires, post, ladder, got to his house, found nobody home and decided it was too late to go to the doctor. He waited until morning, suffered mad pains, and was scolded by the physician for waiting so long. The right wrist was broken in five places.

"I was a little weak from the accident," admitted Ralph modestly, "and stayed in bed for a couple of days. As I lay there, I gradually became aware that my back wasn't hurting any more!

"When I got up, I realized it convincingly—my back really didn't hurt. Not one bit!"

Ralph couldn't understand what had happened. He tried to reason it out. He had fallen, on frozen ground, hard. Somehow the fall must have fused the vertebrae, or whatever they were called, that had been damaged by excessive weight of that platform back in Lantana. If they hadn't been fused, something else had happened to them. Anyway, his back didn't hurt any more.

Later, Ralph submitted to more X-rays at the Red Wing clinic, which still had his original pictures, for comparison.

Although doctors dislike, or refuse, to be quoted, it is no secret that Ralph Samuelson had made some sort of medical history, which was later confirmed at the famous Mayo Clinic.

The backbone, according to theory, could only have been mended with an operation—an operation Ralph had shunned because a friend who had submitted to one was never the same afterward. Yet, this backbone had been healed.

The fall, allegedly, had done what an operation would have tried to do, without any guarantee of absolute success.

The X-rays showing that his back was cured were among Ralph's most precious possession, esteemed almost as highly as his water skis.

"To me it was just more evidence proving how God can take what seemingly is a tragedy and turn it into a great blessing," said Ralph, commenting on the first pain-free nights he had for decades.

"For 30 years I had suffered. Then the good Lord said, I had suffered enough. He let me fall off that pole. It was painful, but the wrist healed fast. So here I am, with a cured back.

"It's a puzzle doctors can't explain. They shouldn't try. I don't."

43. KICKED OUT

The year was up. Ready or not, Ralph Samuelson had to move his family to Pine Island, scenic little town in a bend of the road.

The name, Pine Island, brings a smile to the face of every gourmet who knows anything about cheese.

For from Pine Island came the finest. Good reason. The town was settled by the Swiss, back in 1855. They brought their secrets of cheese making to their new home, Pine Island, a translation of the Sioux word Wa-zu-wee-ta, Isle of Pines. A forest of tall pines on a narrow strip of land on the south side of the Zumbro River. It does look like a green island in a sea of white snow in winter.

It lies perfectly placed and very peacefully where it was founded, gently bypassed by scenic Highway 52, one of the more heavily traveled roads in the state. The route was a much-used inland trail even before the Swiss used it to bring their equipment overland from La Crosse and Madison, Wisconsin.

Pine Island was a busy little town when the Samuelsons moved there, boasting of some industry, fine public schools, with a new $800,000 junior-senior high school building, a fine Van Horn Public Library, six churches, including the one where Ralph had first seen Hazel. It welcomed Ralph and his family as they moved into their new home on Second Avenue, tucked away among tall oaks and elms and cottonwoods, a plain, but neat ranch-cottage type, with a small, heated garage, a garden and room for a kennel and a few boats in the back.

In spite of the welcome, August 20, 1962, is a date the family would rather forget.

Ralph, with a growing capacity for understatement, summarized that heart-breaking departure from his dream house: "It soon came time for us to leave the farm. Our good friend and neighbor LaVerne Windhorst moved our belongings with his large truck, and several other neighbors helped also, as some of our things were heavy, like the piano and the stove.

"I managed to sell our power mower and water heater to LaVerne, and I left the farm with $200 in cash. Not very much when you have a wife and three children to care for.

"I had a funny feeling leaving everything behind me—a whole life's work and savings, a farm and buildings worth roughly speaking $250,000—a quarter of a million in property alone.

"I still had my arm in a cast from the accident that broke my wrist. Later in Pine Island, after the cast was removed, I was offered a job working for the Minnesota Highway Department. I accepted and went to work."

Hazel won't even say that much. To her, the heartbreak was too deep. She didn't care to go back to the house.

As for Ralph, impossible as it may seem, he was still hanging on to that knot at the end of the rope.

"I lived by faith in God's providence. At times it seemed that was all I had to live by too."

And again God came through with a miracle.

The woman who had foreclosed died suddenly. That was not the miracle. Before she died, her husband had made her promise that the Samuelson children must be provided for, no matter what else she did.

When her will was read, Karen, Deborah, and Jon Samuelson were given an annual bequeathement of $2,000, from the time they graduated from high school until the age of 25.

Life settled into a groove at Pine Island. Hazel went on teaching; the children did their appointed chores. Ralph worked part-time for the Highway Department and supplemented his limited income by acting as custodian of the school playgrounds.

When he managed to devise a plan to flood part of the river bottom, and provide a skating rink in winter, keeping it properly flooded, he became a hero to hundreds of kids.

One day, a small knock at the door of the neat, clean modern house on Second Avenue called Hazel from her work. It was little Nancy from across the street. The tot gave Hazel's 60-plus husband the compliment of his life.

Said Nancy, age six, "Can Ralph come out and play?"

Hazel, hiding a smile, passed the message on.

Ralph did go out to play with the first-grader, perhaps remembering the time when his own children were six.

"It was the nicest game of hide and seek I had played for years," recalled Ralph.

All of which takes the Samuelson family, and especially Ralph, to July 28, 1963, when his life took a turn into the stretch, the straight-away, approaching what he liked to call the golden wire, the grand climax—planned, he said, by God ever since he was born.

{7}
Section

44. MARGARET CRIMMINS

If true that God plans everything, his new plan for Ralph Samuelson came in a beautiful package.

An energetic, imaginative, beautiful young journalist, a sports-woman, green-eyed, shapely, who left her hometown of Red Wing, Lake City's neighbor to the north, and worked her way up to the enviable position of Woman's Editor on the *St. Paul Pioneer Press*.

Late in July 1963, Margaret sunbathed on the Lake City beach, run by the very genial Ben Simons, whom Margaret had known for years.

Always eager for a story, even while vacationing, Margaret interrupted her sunbathing and wandered into the bathhouse to get some refreshments and chat with Ben. If you could ever get him to stand still long enough, he sometimes had some fascinating bit of human-interest news, historical or current.

Margaret Crimmins saw the skis before she saw Ben. There

they were, on the wall—two pine slabs, painted white, with big leather straps.

Margaret, an excellent skier herself, stood transfixed. Ben came in. The conversation and the actions that followed Margaret recorded in the next Sunday's *Pioneer Press*, dated July 28, 1963. It appeared in the department "One Woman's View," with Margaret's byline and the headline:

"Your Old Water Skis Are Okay Mr. Samuelsen—Mr. Samuelsen?"

Why and how the spelling "Samelsen," instead of "Samuelson," nobody cares to explain.

But Margeret's story was so far-reaching for water ski history, that it was later framed and hung over Ralph's famous water skis.

Margaret herself, who later worked for the *Washington Post*, should be honored by all water skiers, for had it not been for her, the life of Ralph Samuelson might still be a slow, uneventful series of uneventful events, and millions of water skiers around the world wouldn't know the truth as they know it today. Namely, that it was Ralph Samuelson who started it all—on Lake Pepin, Minnesota. The text of the article follows ("Samuelson" was misspelled in the article.):

There they were, tacked modestly on the Lake City, Minnesota, municipal bathhouse wall.

Munching (guiltily) a gooey ice cream bar, I asked Ben Simons where those Gargantuan water skis had come from. "Oh," said he casually, "those were made by a man by the name of Ralph Samelson. They're supposed to be the first water skis used in the United States.

"Water skiing really got its start in this country right here," said Simons, gesturing toward, the Lake City harbor, of which he is superintendent.

By this time my ice cream was dribbling down my arm, I'd lost interest in nourishment when there was news in front of my sunburned, vacationing nose. I'd never heard that Jacqueline Kennedy, the Cypress Gardens crew, and other ski devotees owe some thanks to a Lake City man. Some 39 years ago he had the spirit, savvy and plain nerve to skim the waves on the boards.

The French Riviera is usually given as the site for the beginning of water skiing sometime in the 20's.

According to Simons, it was 1924 when Samelson, a debonair, adventurous chap, loaded his eight-foot skis into his racy convertible and took off for Florida, where he put on a one-man show. (He'd tried the slippery slats first on Lake Pepin.)

A small, undated yellowed clipping from an unidentified sports magazine is taped beside Samelson's skis. The letter to the editor, signed by a W.H. Giorge of Minneapolis, disputes the claim that U.S. Water Skiing got its start in California (in 1929). Giorge who is not listed in the Minneapolis directory, says in the letter that he sold the materials for the skis to Samuelson in 1924 and attended a water pageant the following year in Lake City. About 10,000, he adds, were on hand to see Samelson towed around Lake Pepin by an airplane on floats.

"The whole town was pretty excited about it," said Simons. "I remember how I and every kid in town used to cluster around Samelson. He was a real hero!"

Where are you now, Mr. Samelson?

I wish I knew. So do Simons and a lot of other Lake Cityites, who are proud of their native son. Some of your townspeople are certain you are still in the Lake City area.

I'd like to meet you, because I tried your skis.

Just as you must have heard—only more than 39 years ago—I heard comments like "You'll break your leg." "You're going to fall flat on your face." "Hope your hospitalization is good."

I'd like to hear how you got up the first time. Getting the tips of those eight-foot monsters above the water is a trick in itself. And, admittedly, I wondered if the leather straps would release me when I fell. Your careful markings of "left" and "right" usually bring a grin to anyone who notices them.

But there IS a left and right ski. You adroitly made the strap looser to allow for the arch. The stair tread works fine for footing.

How many spills did you have before you were upright and slapping over those rollicking Pepin waves? I had two—before I stood up. And then all I could do was hang on. (One arm still aches when I brush my teeth.) I suppose you learned to flop those boards over the wake.

It's a lot easier skimming along with today's skis, about one-half the length and width of yours.

I found myself thinking about the thrill you must have experienced in being one of the—if not THE—first to ski on water in this country. The two young Lake City boys, Scott Peterson and John Schmidt, who followed me on your skis, had the same rather awed feeling after they climbed back into the boat.

"It just goes to show that you usually miss what's going on in your own home town," commented Schmidt.

"These skis have been in the bathhouse for years and no one has tried them," added Peterson. "I feel as though I went back into history a little today."

Both agreed that they had something to tell their grandchildren. But, most of all, they want to meet you, Mr. Samelson.

There are a lot of details we would like to have you fill in on your experiences. And, who knows, maybe you'd like to try some modern skiing?

Margaret Crimmins, like a good journalist, plays it conservatively. She's not quite sure, in this article, whether Ralph is or is not the first man on skis. (In a later article, just as historic, she gives him full credit as the Father of Water Skiing.)

Perhaps Ben Simons knew where Ralph was at the time. But it made a much more dramatic story to have Margaret ask Ralph "Samelsen," through the public media, to come forward, reveal himself, answer a few questions.

Naturally, Samuelson saw that story in the St. Paul Sunday paper. Did Ralph answer the question, "Samelson, where are you?" He did indeed!

"It was like a voice out of my past," recalled Ralph. "Here I was, in little Pine Island, somewhat of a has-been after my big undertaking as a turkey farmer, occasionally leafing through my memory book, remembering many things: that first day on Lake Pepin—on it; the jump; the speed skiing; the rum running and skiing on the Detroit river; the attempts in Florida; the accident that broke my back; the job with the Berkeys; my first marriage; my second marriage; the births of my children; the agony and trouble at our new house; the bankruptcy, the foreclosure; and now the sedate life in a small town, as a retired, but unsuccessful poultry breeder.

"Now this. Frankly, when I read that article in the *Pioneer Press* that hot Sunday morning in July after we had come home from church, I was hit right between the eyes—hard. I had completely forgotten Ben Simons had taken those skis.

"And now here it was—a direct challenge from a woman I had never met. And I could never resist a challenge.

"I smiled at what they had done to my name. A little wryly, I guess, we all have our vanity. But I sure wasn't going to let this thing pass without doing something about it.

"I called Ben Simons in Lake City. He was still living with his mother on South Oak, where they have a big family house. Ben was a confirmed, bachelor—so we thought—until he married his lovely Rosemary some years later.

"I asked Ben if Margaret was still in Lake City. She was. I made a date for the very next day, drove down, and met Margaret. She was charming. She was full of plans, and questions. I answered as well as I could, gave her some names, some leads.

"Once the ice was broken—rather, once the old water skis had gotten wet again—at least some people began to think back and remember, and wonder if we all had missed something. And eventually things did begin to happen.

Not right away, however. It would be two more full years before Ralph got some of the recognition that had passed him by for 40 years!

45. THE EXCITEMENT

First, Margaret, inquiring reporter that she was, asked for pictures.

Pictures!

Pictures, in 1963, of something that happened 41 years ago?

Ralph remembered the photos his friend Grace Eaton had snapped of him. He had already given Ben a few for display.

Ralph hoped he could find a few more at his home, if they hadn't been discarded in the moving. He also recalled that the *Wabasha County Leader* had pictures of his skiing as far back as 1922. But that newspaper was extinct, and the pictures had probably been discarded.

Margaret had a solution. The Minnesota Historical Society had copies of all newspapers ever printed in the state, including those of the Lake City area.

Ben suggested he and Ralph drive up to St. Paul and visit the sedate Historical Society, next to the Minnesota capitol.

Years later, Robert Wheeler, the man who waited on them that morning at the historical society, was present in Lake City to help celebrate the 50th anniversary of the invention of water skiing and present a historical plaque to the city, making Pepin the birthplace of the sport—officially, an honor the Lake well deserved. Wheeler remembered when an "unassuming, self-effacing man" called on him for records of his first water skiing efforts.

He helped his visitors find the valuable editions of *The Leader*, with an article about Ralph, and two photographs to substantiate it, showing Ralph holding his two gargantuan boards, as Margaret Crimmins called them, and Ralph in action behind Walter Bullocks's seaplane.

The boys had Photostats made of everything, took them home.

The Society even found a copy of the *St. Paul Pioneer Press*, with more pictures of the event at White Bear, during the Kiwanis convention.

Back home, Ralph unearthed a few more old photos, especially one showing him jumping that larded diving platform in 1923.

Much to everybody's satisfaction, the pictures reproduced well. The file was building.

Somebody suggested they contact some organization that centralized and coordinated all water ski activities in the country. Nobody knew exactly where or what it was. Somebody else thought he had heard of a group called national Water Ski Club, or something, with headquarters in Florida somewhere.

And somebody else remembered reading a book by a certain water skier, Walter Prince, in which he quoted an interview with a certain Dick Pope, the man who had something to do with Florida's Cypress Gardens skiing. Pope allegedly had said something about a man called Fred Waller of New York State, who was supposed to have invented water skiing in 1924. The reader remembered the date because it was the year in which he had been born.

But the pictures Ben and Ralph had found were clearly dated 1922 and 1923!

It was an exciting situation. But not exciting enough to induce the Lake City Chamber of Commerce, or anybody else, to pursue the matter—to try and find the correct name of that coordinating water ski organization somewhere in Florida and its address.

Everybody was letting everybody else worry about this ski business—which, after all, wasn't so very important. To the average American citizen, what difference did it make who invented that sport?

And so, for two years, nothing happened. Nothing!

Once more Ralph Samuelson was forgotten, almost.

46. THE DEVELOPMENTS

Nobody seems to know why nothing happened for so long.

Ben Simons, for one, was extremely impatient at the slowness with which events were moving—or not moving.

Ben, of course, realized more than most that the sooner Ralph became famous officially, the sooner reflected glory "would publicize the city's marina, the birthplace of Ralph's first water skiing."

Finally, on September 19, 1965, two years and two months after her first article, Margaret Crimmins did it again, and got events off dead center.

Posterity should recognize her as the Fairy Godmother of Water Skiing. Now working for the "Pioneer Press News Service," she released her second article reads as follows, under the headline:

LAKE CITY DISPUTES FRENCH RIVIERA PATERNAL CLAIM TO WATER SKIING

The plush and wealthy French Riviera has a paternity suit on its hands, unofficially filed by this scenic little southeastern Minnesota town.

The contested offspring, whom the French claim to have fathered, is water skiing. Encyclopedias back up the French, stating that water skiing was spanked into life by the waves of the Riviera in the late 1920's.

Not so, say Lake Citians. And they can produce the man— Ralph W. Samuelson, who, they contend, was the world's first water skier, on Lake Pepin, in 1922, some six years before the French tried it; the skis he made and used from 1922 to 1937; dated newspaper clippings and photos chronicling his US appearance, and witnesses to Samuelson's spectacular one-man water skiing shows.

French explorers, Lake Citians concede, gave Lake Pepin its original name, meaning "Lake of Tears." But they can weep all they want about fathering water skiing. The popular sport was born, Lake Citians insist, right off their shores where the Mississippi widens into Lake Pepin.

A self-confessed, "nut about adventure," Ralph Samuelson first got the idea for water skiing, naturally enough, from skiing on snow.

"I was 18 at the time, and believe me, if there was anything new or dangerous I could figure out, I wanted to try it," Samuelson, a native of Lake City, now living in Pine Island, said.

Lake City Graphic

First he tried snow skis, next barrel staves, "and then I went to the lumber yard and bought two large pine boards for $1 each." He curved the tips of the 15-pound, 8-foot skis by steaming them in boiling water, added sections of rubber floor treading for footing and a simple leather strap for each foot.

"I knew the skis had to be large because we couldn't get much speed—only about 20 miles an hour—from boats of that time," Samuelson said.

Ben Simons, supervisor of the Lake City marina, swimming, skating and tourist area, remembers watching Samuelson day after day trying to do an unheard of thing—ski on water.

"I was one of the many young punks who went down to the lake to watch. Everyone in town thought it was kind of a joke. No one thought he could do it, and if he would get up, the water wouldn't hold him.

"Because we all thought the idea was so impossible, it was really a thrill when he finally did get up and go."

After Samuelson mastered water skiing behind the fastest boat he could locate, criss-crossing constantly to maintain speed—he moved to jumping over lard-greased floats. Holding on to a simple metal ring and a sash cord, he learned to ski one-handed and on one foot, dangling the other.

"My reputation as an eccentric really grew when I started to ski behind a boat with a World War I propeller. You could hear it for 10 miles around, but it would go about 50 or 60 miles an hour," Samuelson said. "One time it caught fire and everyone nearly went crazy."

Samuelson's Sunday afternoon water shows, in which he skied and jumped in every zany position he could dream up, and surfboarded doing a headstand on a backless chair, attracted crowds of thousands from all over the area.

For all his shows Samuelson refused to collect a cent, except for boat motor gas money. Most of the admission proceeds went toward purchasing more land for the Lake City harbor and park area, and for extra facilities such as the city's public bathhouse.

"If it weren't for Samuelson we wouldn't have the large waterfront area we do," Simons commented. The city's municipal harbor and marina, beach, picnic and trailer area will eventually cover about 35 acres, a good share of the property purchased through Samuelson's shows.

In 1925, Walter Bullock, one of Northwest Airline's first pilots and another maverick for his time, went to Lake City with a Curtiss MF flying boat, a World War I surplus boat with wings.

"Bullock and I got together, as two nuts, I guess. He'd carry passengers while I skied. That was really a ride, sometimes as fast as 80 miles an hour," Samuelson recalls.

"We attracted a lot of people because both the flying boat and water skiing were such novelties," commented Bullock during a telephone interview. He now is retired and living in Lakeville, Minn.

Samuelson's leaps from behind Bullock's winged boat were sometimes as high as 50 feet.

"The good Lord must really have been watching over me; I was never hurt, even though I fell and slid once about a quarter of a mile. And I never wore a life preserver. I just never thought about being afraid," said Samuelson, whose bright blue eyes still sparkle like an adventurous youth's.

Admitting he was somewhat of a playboy and showman at the time, Samuelson each fall in the late 20's and early 30's stashed his skis in a fancy yellow roadster and took off for Palm Beach, Fla., to stage his one-man water shows.

Lake City Graphic

"There were many wealthy people from the French Riviera who watched me water ski in Palm Beach. They were fascinated and certainly hadn't seen anything like it before. But I think they took the idea home, and that's how the Riviera got credit as the birthplace of water skiing," Samuelson said.

The article, which ran in the *Sunday Pioneer Press*, was embellished with three photos, one of Ralph as of 1925, holding his skis, taller than himself, standing beside Bullock's Curtiss; a second of Ralph, a la 1965, in a business suit instead of a swimming suit holding the same skis. (The cover photo of this book.)

In this one, taken on a pier in Lake City's marina, with boat shelters in the background, Ben Simons is kneeling beside Samuelson, obviously not to get in the way of the two old boards.

The third is of city officials surveying the area Samuelson's water shows helped to buy: Larry E. Oberg, publisher of the *Lake City Graphic*, head of the Lake City waterfront board which had approved plans for a half-million-dollar harbor, much of it on property purchased through Samuelson's water skiing shows,

Logan Johnson and Dr. Robert Seberg of the Chamber of Commerce.

After that article hit the streets of the lake and river towns of Minnesota and adjoining states, things moved faster.

. The Lake City Chamber, no doubt under the persistent prodding of men like Simons, Oberg, Johnson and Seberg, wrote a letter to the American Water Ski Association.

It was a letter vitally important in the annals of water skiing, today's multi-million dollar sport and industry.

47. THE LETTER

On its official stationery, with the artistic logo, "The Heart of the Fabulous Hiawatha Valley—on Beautiful Lake Pepin," the chamber, still not having the name quite right, addressed a letter to the National Water Ski Association. Ralph had given them the information that the Association was located in Winter Haven, Florida. Said the letter:

Dec. 9, 1965
National Water Ski Association
Winter Haven
Florida

Gentlemen:

We understand, that you're checking out the origin of water skiing.

In 1922, a young daredevil of Lake City skied on Lake Pepin for the first time so far as any of us know. He was a frequent attraction to residents and visitors who could not conceive how his feat was possible.

The skis he used were far different than any used today being about 8 feet long and about 12 inches wide. We have them on display in our office—but are thinking of presenting them to the Smithsonian Institute.

We are happy to have the signatures below, Lake City men who remember and are glad to testify to Ralph Samuelson's water skiing on Lake Pepin in 1922, and many years after that.

Sincerely,
LAKE CITY CHAMBER OF COMMERCE
Robert B. Seberg, President
Charles R. Hoyt
Ralph J. Adolph
Warren Peterson
J.H. Roschen
Harry Olson
Clarence D. Zillgitt
E.R. Saunders
Anita Riester

Most of the signers of that letter, in reality an affidavit, were still active when seven years later, Lake City, the state, and the nation celebrated the 50th anniversary of the invention of water skiing by Ralph Samuelson.

Charles Hoyt, respected owner of Lake City's nationally known flour mill, dating back to the previous century, not only signed the letter but, on many occasions, signed personal checks when the city had to meet emergencies or individuals needed help.

Charles often declared how proud he was of what Ralph had done for the town. The mill office kept a scrapbook of some of Samuelson's activities and featured him in one of their full-page ads in the official milling publication, *The Southwest Miller*.

Charles should remember Ralph, for the future father of water skiing was running the Pepin Lodge II when Charles was courting Mrs. Berkey's niece, Minnesota Comstock, on the top deck.

"We could always depend on him," said Charles, remembering those nights. "When he made a promise, we knew he'd keep it. But he could never turn down a challenge. Lake Pepin challenged him to ski on her, and he did."

Robert Seberg, who signed the historic letter as President of the Chamber, gives much credit to a man who never forced himself to the front, the late Logan Johnson, one of Hoyt's executives, and chairman of the city's Civic, Industrial, and Professional Bureau. He wrote a revealing letter:

> It was when Logan Johnson came to us that real action started, in this project. While many of our citizens were still prejudiced against Samuelson, calling him a "ham," Johnson was not prejudiced against him, and saw the good it could do for Lake City and the State of Minnesota, if we could prove that Ralph Samuelson was the real Father of Water Skiing. He had the time, the enthusiasm, and the facilities to get the job done.
>
> I signed the letter to the AWSA because I was Chamber President at the time. When Ralph was named Father of Water Skiing, and the subsequent celebration was planned, I was appointed Chairman of the event by Herb Hinck, then Chamber president.
>
> Samuelson was always very cooperative, went to the TV and radio stations at our request. To my knowledge we never gave him any money for doing this. We were convinced Ralph was the real Father of Water Skiing when we sent the letter. But we were not sure we would be accepted by others. Naturally, I thought more would come of the acceptance than has up to now.
>
> I believe Samuelson has more friends here now than ever before because of his unselfish attitude in promoting Lake City along with being the Father of Water Skiing. There are still some who consider him a ham, however.

Bob Seberg, prominent dental surgeon of Lake City for 16 years, later became chairman of the Goodhue County Planning and Zoning Commission, and worked into the 1970s to make more people realize that Lake City actually is the birthplace of water skiing.

The late Wilmer (Tony) Strickland, then in his fourth term as mayor of Lake City, wrote on official stationery:

> As mayor of Lake City, where it all began, and where we celebrated the 50th anniversary of the Birth of Water Skiing a couple

of years ago, I feel compelled to say the town owes Ralph Samuelson something for starting it all.

I've known Ralph all my life and I can remember his many exploits here on Lake Pepin. Water skiing is now one of the major sports of Lake City.

Tony wasn't one of the original signers of the official Chamber letter, but he signed many letters later, promoting both Samuelson and Lake City, until his tragic death as a murder victim.

A man who did sign the document was Warren R. Peterson, retired owner of a funeral service in its third generation, still living in the block where he was born. He recalled the entire Samuelson clan, personally went ice boating and power boating with them in the old days, and witnessed Ralph's early water skiing maneuvers.

Warren remembered that the favorite sport for the waterfront gang was the old powerhouse near the Lake, located at the identical spot where Margaret Crimmins later discovered Ralph' old skis. Peterson wrote:

> At the time I signed the affidavit, I was attending a meeting of the Lake City Water and Light Board in our old City Hall. I was selected because of my many years in Lake City, and the association with the Samuelson family, actually seeing the start of water skiing on Lake Pepin.
>
> Little did we know at that time that a young man's dream would end up as a favorite world-wide sport, and that it would help to make Lake City and Lake Pepin what it is today, with the marina, sail boats of all sizes, and the multitude of people who are attracted to the natural beauty of our environment.
>
> Water skiing and its history have been a big factor in the advertisement of this beauty spot.

J.H. Roschen, another signer, recalled the days vividly when he occasionally watched Ralph try to get on top of Lake Pepin's waves with his homemade skis. The retired general manager of the Lake City Farmer Elevator was involved in local government for more than 30 years, serving as councilman, charter commissioner, planning commissioner, and member of the Water and Light Board. He said:

> The popularity of the sport, and the publicity it received, prompted me to sign the Chamber of Commerce letter of December 9, 1965, with the feeling that it would promote Lake City as a great recreational area.
>
> My hopes have indeed been justified. I am proud that I could help to bring it about.

Another signer, Ralph J. Adolph, "Zump" to his friends, represented a family closely associated with Lake City. Zump first dispensed his fragrant, buttered popcorn at the historic water carnivals, later sold it at a fixed location in town. By this time it was called atomic popcorn. Zump retired in 1973. He wrote:

> I remember signing that letter to the American Water Ski Association. And the reason I did is fairly obvious.
>
> I was interested enough in the community and in what Ralph had done, to see to it that he got the proper recognition I felt was due him.
>
> I had been one of the first, if not the first operator and lifeguard at the old wooden bathhouse, then at the end of the Lake City Point. I believe this building was donated to the city by the McCahill family, true pioneers who were always interested in what was good for the community. This took place about 1915 or 1917, as I entered the Navy in 1917.
>
> The second bathhouse was built where the present one is now. It was underwritten by the Lake City Commercial Club, a predecessor of the present Chamber of Commerce. Water shows, pageants, speedboat races were held to pay for it.
>
> I took part in some of those shows by doing a hobo-clown routine with my friend, Donald Pletch, who acted on stilts. Ralph

Samuelson appeared on many shows. I watched him and Red Walstrom practice their routines on many occasions—first behind a launch, then behind a contraption driven by an airplane engine.

I thought then, as I do now, that Ralph Samuelson did a tremendous job of putting our town on the map.

I was especially thrilled when I watched him being pulled behind Captain Bullock's airplane.

I remember an occasion when Tommy Bartlett [of later Wisconsin Dells water skiing and promotion fame] came to Lake City to book one of his Cypress Gardens exhibitions.

He told us that water skiing had originated in France. I disagreed with him, and told him that it had been born right here in Lake City; and that someday Ralph Samuelson's efforts would be proved a fact. This has now come to pass to our great satisfaction.

Clarence Zillgitt, retired postmaster of Lake City, who became more active than ever after leaving his post office, made valuable remarks about that Chamber letter which he signed:

Why did I sign the letter?

I had several reasons. First, of course, is the basic fact that I did witness Samuelson perform on his homemade skis in 1922 and could so attest.

Further, the action on my part was the result of a general desire to support public credit for this man due to his unusual achievement. Probably, however, it resulted in a greater degree from my civic pride and the attending wish that his accomplishment bring favorable publicity to the community of Lake City. Finally, in all honesty, I must confess that the opportunity for me to share Samuelson's recognition, even though only in a small measure, was a factor influencing signing the letter.

How well did I know Samuelson back in 1922?

Born in Lake City, Samuelson and I, at early ages,. were exposed to swimming and other water activities at the local bathing beach near the old power house. Throughout summer seasons, we were present there almost daily and became well acquainted, although Ralph was a year and a half older than I. In 1922, the year of

Ralph's great adventure, I not only watched him perform, but often talked to him, very often discussed matters pertaining to his water ski performances with their attending problems.

Did I feel the AWSA acknowledgment helped Lake City?

The AWSA acknowledgment helped Lake City to the extent that the city's location became known not only nationally, but in numerous foreign countries as well. While this did not in any substantial degree reflect in local business profits, it did bring a remarkable distinction to the community.

Did I believe Samuelson would ever be acknowledged nationally?

I did not. During his early skiing years, I never knew of any action being taken by anyone, including Samuelson himself, to gain recognition. Margaret Crimmins, *St. Paul Pioneer Press* writer, actually opened the door when, purely by accident and during a trip to Lake City looking for news, she discovered Samuelson's skis and received an account of their significance from Ben Simons, local bathing beach manager. Thereafter Logan Johnson and other Chamber of Commerce people deserve credit for promotion, resulting in national recognition.

My feelings about the whole thing today?

How the events of past years remain indelibly impressed in my mind. As I continue to reflect on them, I'm of the deep conviction that, all in all, the efforts of many people concerned with this historical event, paid off in an impressive manner.

Harry Olson, a lifetime friend of Samuelson, remembered much:

Back in the early '20s, when I was a teenager, activity on Lake Pepin was pretty much limited to earning a living. Clamming and fishing was a valued industry in the summertime, and in the winter the ice on the lake provided a bridge for Wisconsin farmers to haul wood, hay and grain to the market at Lake City. Ice was also harvested and stored in sawdust in a large ice house near the City Point to be used by consumers for their ice boxes the following summer.

A few launches (inboard motor boats) were used for pleasure and ran faster than the majority of boats on the lake. Ralph Samuelson's father had such a boat, and did a thriving business clamming in summer. From the clams they obtained pearls, and the shells were sold to the local button factory, where I worked for a while as a boy,

The Samuelsons lived a short distance from my parent's home, and of course we knew the family well. Our house, which fronted Lake Pepin, was a constant site from which we could watch all the water activities.

Bach Sunday afternoon relatives and friends from out of town would gather on our front porch and lawn, hoping to get a glimpse of Ralph performing a neat feat on Pepin.

First he used a surfboard behind a boat; then he perched himself on a chair on the surf board; and finally his greatest performance was initiating a pair of skis into his act.

We were not the only admirers, as many people would gather in the park, awaiting this weekly water show.

Surprisingly, no one else attempted this feat for many years. He provided many hours of entertainment for us, and many others, and his stunts were considered daring and risky.

We now feel honored that this water skiing so long ago should bring recognition to our city. We feel rightfully proud of our native son.

The only woman to sign that affidavit was Miss Anita Riester, who, together with the late E.A. Saunders, did so because of their personal friendship with Ralph Samuelson.

Anita saw Ralph ski often in 1922, and saw him make some of his big jumps of 50 and 60 feet, much to the amazement of the spectators.

For many years an employee of the Silver Sail Cafe, of which Saunders was the owner, Anita recalled the days when Ralph would drop in for lunch and a visit. Said Anita:

Ralph Samuelson's water sport programs attracted thousands of people to Lake City, which helped business, including our cafe, and did so much for our bathing beach, which is now one of the most popular recreation centers of southern Minnesota. We are very happy to recognize him as the first water skier on record.

Anita signed the Chamber letter because she felt Ralph had brought much recognition to her city, and this was a small personal favor she could do for him and for his spirit of adventure.

Slowly thus the stage was being set for a new act in Ralph Samuelson's drama of life.

Whether he was as impatient about the slow pace as some others, he does not divulge.

But then, he was going through developments of his own, he insists—developing greater patience, more tolerance, developing greater faith—and letting that faith show.

Had nothing happened, had Ralph Samuelson never received the recognition which was now creeping up on him ever so slowly, he probably would have shrugged it all off by saying God didn't want him to have any recognition."

But recognition came with a whoop and a holler!

48. THE RECOGNITION

In the December-January 1966 issue of its official publication *The Water Skier*, the American Water Ski Association finally committed itself.

A slug on the front cover teased the reader with the announcement, "Water Skiing Has a New 'Real Father' P.36." The AWSA not only published verbatim the letter from the Lake City Chamber of Commerce, but carried a boxed editorial and an article by Margaret Crimmins, plus four photographs.

When asked to summarize, as much as possible, the steps that eventually led the Association to give Samuelson the recognition that had passed him by for so long, Thomas C. Hardman, editor and publisher of the magazine wrote the following letter:

As to the timetable, I can't help you prior to the fall of 1965 since we knew nothing of Margaret Crimmins' 1963 article. We first heard of Samuelson when one of our association members in the St.

Paul area forwarded a clipping to us anonymously from the *Pioneer Press*. From your notes, this was the writer's second article.

I reached Margaret Crimmins by telephone and arranged for her to write a more complete story for *The Water Skier* and obtained from her Ralph Samuelson's telephone number in Pine Island. In a conversation with him, I verified much of the information and arranged to borrow some of his early photographs for reproduction purposes.

Meanwhile, we obtained additional verification of the facts from the Lake City Chamber of Commerce in the form of the letter, which was published with our initial article in The Water Skier. Without going back in our storage files, I don't recall whether the chamber letter was solicited by us or whether it was simply forwarded to us after chamber officials learned of our interest. As memory serves, I suspect the latter was the case.

The boxed editorial, still a bit cautious, stated:

Just when all concerned on both aides of the Atlantic were about willing to accept the late Fred Waller of Huntington, N.Y. as the real "father of water skiing", up comes a semi-retired Minnesota turkey farmer who now appears to have started the whole thing way back in 1922, three years before Waller patented his famed "Akwa-Skees," and two years before he ever tried them. Frank W. Samuelson, now 62, and living in Pine Island, Minnesota, successfully attempted to ski on water, the conventional way, when he was 18 years old at Lake City— a fact recently uncovered by Margaret Crimmins, a newspaper writer for the *St. Paul Pioneer Press*. Here, as she wrote "The Water Skier," is how her discovery came about:

"Actually Samuelson's claim to fathering water skiing never would have been made if I hadn't taken a vacation in Lake City. One day I went into the bathhouse and saw his strange looking skis on display. I then asked the manager, Ben Simons, if I could try them out for a story for the *Pioneer Press*. He agreed and said he believed they were the first ever, but no one had ever done anything about making any claims. So I rode on them, and the column I did for the St. Paul paper turned up Samuelson at his home in Pine Island.

"Then the whole city got excited, and Samuelson was brought in for a sort of impromptu celebration. This gave me the background for a more complete story for the newspaper and this version in *The Water Skier.*

"As for the skis. It was a wild experience on them. I plopped twice but got up on the third try behind a 40-horsepower rig. The skis were really difficult to hold together because of their length. Two teenage boys went out with me. One got up and skied for a short distance (about a hundred yards just as I had done), but the other never did make it."

Aside from calling Ralph, "Frank," and stating that the fact of his existence had "recently" been uncovered, when as a matter of fact it was two and a half years since Margaret wrote her first article about him and his skis, the editorial is certainly a shining marker in the history of water skiing.

The piece Margaret Crimmins wrote for the same issue of *The Water Skier*, at the request of the editor, is an augmented, more detailed rewrite of her 1965 story in the *Pioneer Press*, intended for a more specialized audience, to most of whom her information was new, and thrilling, even though a few dates in it don't jibe with those given by Ralph later. It began:

While a friendly argument on the origin of water skiing persisted for years, a modest Minnesota man stayed quietly in the background, content in the belief that he actually was the first water skier.

Margaret ends the article with a reference to Ralph Samuelson's strong religious convictions.

After that publication came out, events speeded up. On February 18 of that same year, 1966, William P. Barlow, Jr., the President of the American Water Ski Association, wrote a formal answer to Dr. Robert Seberg, President of the Lake City Chamber of Commerce:

Dr. Dr. Seberg:

While the recognition of Lake City as the birthplace of water skiing has been a long time in coming, it is my pleasure now, as President of the American Water Ski Association, to recognize Mr. Ralph W. Samuelson as the first water skier of record known to our association, and to congratulate Lake City, Minnesota, as the scene of Mr. Samuelson's pioneering activity in our sport.

Water skiing, like so many other discoveries, was apparently the independent brainchild of a number of adventuresome people both in this country and in Europe. As a result, the sport has had a number of inventors over the years, but Mr. Samuelson's development in 1922 easily precedes all other known claimants.

It is not often that a sport which attracts more than 9,000,000 Americans annually, and which has spread throughout the world as a major recreational activity, is able to recognize and honor its founder. I was, along with thousands of other members of the American Water Ski Association, intensely interested in the account of Mr. Samuelson's early water skiing and your letter attesting to this accomplishment, which appeared in the current issue of our official publication *The Water Skier*, under the by-line of Margaret Crimmins.

This published account represents the newly discovered milestone in the history of the fastest-growing family sport in America. Mr. Samuelson and his former hometown of Lake City can be justly proud of their role in its origin.

Very truly yours,

Wm. P. Barlow, Jr., President

Two months later, on April 22, 1966, William D. Clifford, Executive Manager of the American Water Ski Association, made it even more official when he wrote directly to Ralph Samuelson in Pine Island:

Dear Mr. Samuelson:

One of the most significant developments in organized water skiing for many years had been the "rediscovery" of your pioneering activities in the sport, as reported in the December-January 1966, issue of our official publication. *The Water Skier*. It is my real pleasure to recognize you as the first water skier of record known to the American Water Ski Association, and to salute you in the name of the sport that now attracts more than 9,000,000 participants each year in America alone.

It has been particularly interesting for me to note from the many early photographs and newspaper accounts, which you have permitted us to borrow, that your water skiing in 1922 took on substantially the same form that it has today, with free skis and a towline attached directly to the towboat.

Your leaping on skis off a ramp and "speed skiing" behind an amphibious aircraft also likely represents "first" in phases of water skiing that heretofore have been regarded as much more recent in origin.

We welcome you as an honorary life member of the American Water Ski Association and look forward to the time that you will be able to visit our National Headquarters and to attend one of our annual membership meetings. I am sure that many of our members whose skiing dates back to the Twenties and Thirties will be most interested in looking back with you to "the good old days."

Let me know if we can be of service.

William D., Clifford Executive Manager.

To put the entire, bizarre story of the paternity suit of water skiing, as Margaret Crimmins called it, into even better perspective, it is only necessary to quote a letter written a few months after Clifford, and to refer to a few other gems from water ski archives.

The letter is from Charles R. Sligh, a furniture manufacturer from Holland, Michigan, former president of the Association, who watched water skiers at the New York's World's Fair in 1939 and took the idea back to the Midwest.

Sligh's letter, dated June 14, 1966, is also addressed to Samuelson:

My face is red for not having written you long ago to congratulate you for having started my favorite sport. I started skiing just seventeen years after you invented the sport and have been skiing ever since. It has meant much to both me and my family and I am only sorry that I have not had the opportunity to meet you and also that you have not received more recognition for the part you played in water skiing many years ago.

At the time I was president of the American Water Ski Association I ran articles in the *Water Skier* magazine asking for any information, which might be available concerning the originator of the sport. The earliest documentary evidence we received had to do with Fred Waller, and his patented skis in 1923 (actually 1925), and for that reason of course he has been given credit for many years for being the originator of water skiing as well as of Cinerama.

I am pleased that evidently we have now found the true originator of water skiing and hope that your future part in the sport will give you much satisfaction and pleasure.

I read with interest the various letters carried in the April-May issue of *The Water Skier* and it is because of this that I am writing to you now.

With every good wish.

Cordially,

Chuck Charles B. Sligh, Jr.

The articles and letters Sligh refers to were dug out of storage morgues. They go back to January 1952, all of 14 years before Samuelson stepped into the limelight.

They tell an often tongue-in-cheek story of wrangling about the originator of water skiing even at that date. Two cities, Seattle, Washington, and Winter Haven, Florida, got into a pseudo-altercation about claiming the honor as the original home of the sport. It seems, the whole argument at the time, 1952, began with a national radio program, in pre-television days.

The Water Skier appeared to settle the feud between the two cities when it published a letter written by Fred Waller of New York City, who was then proclaimed to be the Father of Water Skiing. The magazine wrote:

"While all these other people [in Seattle, Winter Haven and elsewhere] were delving into the intricacies of building water skis which would work and be comfortable to ride, it was all rather old stuff to Fred Waller of New York City. If you don't believe us, here's his story. As further proof we ask that you please take a good look at the advertisement which Fred ran way back in 1925 in connection with his water skis in an effort to get more venturous souls out of their arm chairs and unto the water—not in it necessarily, although they tell us, that usually follows!

Here then is Fred Waller's letter:

"I first rode on water skis of my own design behind my boat in Long Island Sound in 1924.

As a result, I applied for a patent on Water Skis and this was granted in 1925 (US Patent No. 1559390).

"Unfortunately, two of the people who were with me on the boat when I made my first test are dead, and the third is out of the country, so I can't furnish affidavits.

I rode both types of skis; the ones on which the rider holds onto the rope and has skis fastened to the boat, and the type which I first put on the market under the name of Dolphin Akwa-Skees, in which each one was towed by a rope connecting to a bridle which was pulled by the single tow rope from the bow end of each ski was attached a hand rope so that the boat pulled the skis the way it does in aquaplane. The reason for putting this type on the market was that they are very much easier to ride.

Fred Waller

A picture below the article, showing an attractively buxom lass in the act of skiing, has the caption:

"Picture below is from the collection owned by Dan Haines. Shows Annette Webster, using Fred Waller's patented direct-tow water skis. These skis have no bindings, only rubber foot pads. Annette is skiing in the open ocean off Atlantic City Steel Pier—regular daily shows—about 1935 or 1936.

The same issue of *The Water Skier* carries the advertisement of the Dolphin Akwa-Skees, two boys and a girl holding them up for display. Under the picture is the caption:

> "Here's Fred Waller's advertisement—an absolute copy. Shows his skis which he patented in 1925 (US Patent No. 1559390). We give in—we're convinced that Fred beat both Seattle and Winter Haven to water skis. Do you give up? If not—we'll expect to hear from you—with proof—of course."

That was, obviously, the time when the water ski world and its officials should have heard from Ralph Samuelson who could prove he had skied two years earlier than Waller!

They didn't. Not for another 13 years. Why? Apparently neither Ralph nor anybody else in Lake City read *The Water Skier*, at least not this historic issue.

The "various letters" Sligh refers to in his June 14, 1966, letter to Samuelson, appeared in the Letterbox of the May-April 1966 issue of *The Water Skier*, after Samuelson had been acknowledged as the true father of the sport. The editor himself has a preface to the four letters:

> Correspondence has been flying thick and fast since the publication in our December-January 1966 issue of the feature "Water Skiing has a new 'Real Father'" which told of Ralph Samuelson first getting up on conventional type water skis at Lake City, Minnesota, in 1922. The Lake City Chamber of Commerce, and more recently, the State of Minnesota have begun publicity programs which are paying belated tribute to Mr. Samuelson.
>
> Johnson Motors had him as the company's guest at the Chicago Regional Boat, Travel & Outdoor show in March (Mr. Samuelson raced Johnson engines back in the early thirties). Plans are now underway for Mr. Samuelson to make an exhibition tour, skiing for the first time in nearly 30 years. Following are excerpts from a few of the letters and copies of letters that have crossed the editor's desk in the past several months.

The first letter is the one Barlow sent to Dr. Seberg, already mentioned. The second is from that same Don Ibsen of Seattle, who was once acclaimed by his city as the inventor of water skiing. He wrote to Ralph Samuelson:

Dear Ralph:

Congratulations on the fine article and photographs in *The Water Skier*. My story is similar to yours, as I was 19 in 1928 when I made my first water skis. I also built early jump ramps, floated with truck innertubes, put on shows for the public, newsreels, papers and magazines. I skied behind a Savio Marchetti Italian flying boat at 70 miles an hour when I was younger and more daring.

Many have billed me as "the father of water skiing," but since I heard from Fred Waller and his bridled Akwa Skees being invented in 1925, I say I am one of the early pioneers. I do believe I have continuously been more active in all facets of the sport than anyone else for 37 years. I doubt that many pioneers 55 years of age have mastered the water ski hydrofoils, and still carry people in the arms on their shoulders on one ski, etc.

When I have discussed the origin of water skiing, I have often said that others will crop up as the years go by. I wonder why I never heard about you when my sister and I toured 25 states promoting the sport in 1940? We met Chuck Sligh of Holland, Mich., and came back with three others from Seattle in 1941 to the Nationals on Lake Macatawa. At that tournament I won third in tricks—"a Jack Knife" with the daring high-point trick, holding the towline in my mouth while riding one ski and holding the other with my hand. Thank goodness water skiing has come a long way since then.

Regardless of by whom and when water skiing was first invented, I feel all pioneers who started it in their localities should band together, and the AWSA should initiate a Water Skiing Hall of Fame. It will be a real pleasure if we can meet some day and talk over old times. It's too bad Fred Waller is not around to visit with us.

Don Ibsen, Class of 1928.

Ibsen and Samuelson finally did meet in Seattle, but not until

1972, six years later. And the hoped-for Hall of Fame became a reality in 1976.

The next letter in the Letterbox was one Ralph Samuelson wrote to Don Ibsen:

Dear Don:

I was very pleased to receive your letter and hope we can get together some day to compare our experiences of early water skiing.

I started in 1922 and had to quit due to a broken back, which I received in an accident in Florida while working on a building project.

I have never had a pair of water skis on since that day. I guess that's why you haven't heard of me until now. You probably wouldn't have heard of me at all if Margaret Crimmins (author of the article published in *The Water Skier*) had not discovered my early water skis hanging on the wall of the public bathhouse in Lake City. She started to ask questions and finally after getting old newspaper clippings and pictures, we could prove without doubt that I started water skiing way back in 1922.

I am inclosing a souvenir of my early water skiing, back in 1925 when I started jumping and when I took my first ride behind an aeroplane. I am glad to hear that there were other nuts besides myself doing this sort of thing—meaning you, of course! The skis in the picture were not the ones used behind the plane. This was an old picture taken in 1924, but the newspaper used it for the seaplane story.

Ralph Samuelson

Pine Island

The final letter indicates that even before the 1966 adulation in Lake City, which Ralph got later, he did receive a bit of attention. In a letter to Tom Hardman he writes:

Dear Tom:

I have a great deal to tell you about what happened after I came home from the boat show in Chicago. I was called to come to the State Office Building in St. Paul and visited the Director of Publicity and Promotion, They want me to travel the boat shows next winter, the same as I did in Chicago, and I expect to cover all the principal cities in the US.

I am riding water skis again at Lake City, Minn, on July 3, to celebrate my birthday. I will have to do a little practice as I have not been on water skis for about 30 years, since I broke my back in Florida. I also broke my wrist in a fall from a light pole, but my back was miraculously healed at the same time so there is no apparent reason why I can't ski again, although it won't be behind an airplane!

Recently I was invited to give a talk on early water skiing at the Prior Lake Ski Club. I received a royal welcome and an engraved plaque as the first water skier. I think about 100 people were present, and after my talk I received five minutes of applause. It made me feel very humble.

Four members of my family will be riding water skis this summer. It will be pretty exciting to see my children ride as they have never tried it before.

Ralph Samuelson

Pine Island.

A sidelight on the speech before the Prior Lake Club. It was the first time Ralph got that kind of applause, his first public acclaims as the father of water skiing. Even then, he accepted it with humility and gratitude.

It is interesting to note that Ralph took his children skiing for the first time that summer. When Karen was then 17, Debbie 15, Jon 14, they learned fast and became champion water skiers. They should be. They had about the best instructor available.

Ralph made one other comment about that historic May 1966, issue of *The Water Skier*, which carried the Letterbox. In it appears an ad promoting kites for flying, which, according to the caption, were flown by the first three finishers in slalom, tricks and overall during the previous National Kite Flying Championship Competition in water skiing.

Water skiing had taken to the air, even had its own champions. When he saw the ad, Ralph grinned wryly, claimed ruefully that in a way he was not only the first skier, the first jumper, the first speed king, but also the first flying skier. Back in 1925 Walter Bullock's old plane had yanked him bodily off the water of Lake Pepin.

"At least I felt I was flying, until I dropped. Then I was only belly skiing," he added with a laugh. "Many must have belly skied since then. But I guess I was the first in that, too."

In his letter giving the chronological steps that led to Ralph's recognition, Hardman also says:

> We were careful to refer to Samuelson as "the first water skier on record" since Fred Waller had long been accorded this distinction on both sides of the Atlantic, and we had no way of knowing whether another "Ralph Samuelson" might suddenly crop up. We still don't, but the possibility grows increasingly remote as time goes on.

Tom Hardman ends his letter with one of the most sincere, simple, and convincingly compelling compliments any skier has ever received—one that describes Ralph Samuelson well:

> If we had a way of foreordaining these things, organized water skiing couldn't have picked a finer "father" than Ralph Samuelson. He has been a real asset in promoting the sport since his "discovery" a dozen years ago, largely because of his modesty and his genuine wonderment at what he started quite innocently back in 1922.

Describing Ralph Samuelson as "modest, full of genuine wonderment at what he started" puts it all in less than 10 words.

That wonderment remained a part of Samuelson's philosophy, although it was more than human wonderment. Ralph wondered at the mysterious ways God chose, to bring about results He thinks are important.

"Sure, I'm amazed and experience wonderment every time I see a water ski exhibition, at what I started. But I also feel and know more and more every year, that I merely did what God intended me to do right along. Not only to give the world a new sport, a sport which is really just now beginning to work out its potentials, but to get ready to tell my story—a story full of gratitude to the good Lord, and full of hope for mankind, in spite of all the tribulations and troubles we have in the world today. I must tell the whole suffering world that we will never fulfill our purpose on this earth until we are reborn, and let the Holy Spirit work on us, as he did on me."

What about Hardman's idea that the Association has no way of knowing whether another Ralph Samuelson might suddenly crop up, Ralph was asked.

He had a ready answer: "It's as Mr. Hardman says, the possibility of another Father of Water Skiing cropping up grows increasingly remote. But if one does appear, I'll turn my crown over with grateful appreciation for the past years, when it was my privilege to help not only the sport of water skiing, but my country, my state, my town, and my Lake as much as possible, by representing them as well as I possibly could. It was a challenge, and as you know, I could never turn down a challenge."

49. THE ACCLAIM

When, in 1966, Lake City's enthusiasm finally went public, it did so with a will.

First, it proclaimed its own special "Father's Day," setting it for June 19, the nation's regular Father's Day.

The event was reminiscent of old times when the whole town cooperated feverishly to put on one of its water carnivals, or Fourth of July parades.

This time there was a new excitement, and a more pervading purpose behind it all, for Lake City, the little town by the Lake, which had been only a wooding stop for side-wheelers and stern-wheelers, was becoming famous, nationally.

True, its reputation had already gone beyond its own borders to some extent. The trees and shrubs and flowers of the Jewell Nursery, where Ralph Samuelson pulled all those weeds, had been sent to many parts of the country. And the Golden Loaf Flour of the century-old Tennant and Hoyt Mill was used by bakers in many states. Foundry products from the local foundry had carried the name of Lake City.

But it had never been noticed by the entire sports world as it was now.

For the American Water Ski Association, highest authority for the lusty, splashing new sport, had officially acknowledged it as the Birthplace of Water Skiing; and its native son as the real Father.

Never before had the town been challenged so openly to take its light out from under the bushel and let it shine.

And it accepted the challenge, even as Ralph Samuelson had accepted the challenge of his Lake.

Almost every organization in town jumped in to do its share—the Chamber, the Junior Chamber, Kiwanis, the schools, the churches, the Woman's Club, the Garden Clubs, the Country Club, the VFW, the Legion, various other groups.

And it was mostly done with love and care and professional enthusiasm, almost as if people were making up for lost time.

Invitations were mailed to each town along the whole Hiawatha-Pioneer Trail, all up and down the river, to send a band, a float, a queen, a car, preferably a boat, to the June 19 celebration honoring Ralph Samuelson.

A committee of the Chamber met in Red Wing with representatives of the Hiawatha-Pioneer Council, to discuss ways and means. They invited the State Department of Business Development to participate. The Department accepted. They planned a boat parade, a water ski show, band concerts, a teen dance. They called on Walter Bullock, who agreed to fly down in one of his reconstructed 1908 planes.

The American Water Ski Association promised to send a man to present Samuelson with a beautiful trophy, donated by the

Chamber. A native celebrity, Richard Hoyt, son of Ralph's friend, Chuck Hoyt, a military parachutist, promised to do parachute jump; a queen was selected, beautiful Charlyne Wold, 18, the 1966 All-Girl-Athlete of Lincoln High School. She appeared before TV cameras and on radio in the Twin Cities and other places to promote the event.

Press kits were dispatched to every newspaper in the area—and to sports editors of papers in Chicago, Milwaukee, St. Louis, and the Twin Cities.

The advance publicity granted by the media was amazing. Complete stories of Ralph Samuelson, his accomplishments, the history of water skiing were featured in papers like the *Milwaukee Journal*, in sports magazines, Sunday supplements, weeklies.

The Prior Lake Ski Team was engaged to put on a water show.

Even the Associated Press sent a man who took and circulated pictures of the beautiful Charlyne bussing the newly discovered Father of Water Skiing.

The Fairy Godmother, Margaret Crimmins, and the Power Behind it All, Ben Simons, were photographed time and again. Vice President Hubert H. Humphrey sent a letter:

Dear Mr. Samuelson:

I noticed where you have been honored by the American Water Ski Association as "father of water skiing." Congratulations on receiving this fine recognition. You have certainly provided the nation with a fine and healthy sport and are deserving of our thanks.

Best wishes.

Hubert H. Humphrey

It all came off as planned, with hoopla and an enthusiasm reserved for small towns that don't become surfeited with too many events chasing each other.

The Lake City Graphic, in the next edition, Thursday, June 23, 1966, front-paged the event with photos of "The Throngs Estimated as up to 10,000 Persons," pictures of Howard Viken, master of ceremonies, popular WCCO-Twin Cities radio personality talking to Richard Hoyt, the parachutist, and of the big three, Ralph, Margaret, and Ben.

Said *The Graphic*, summing it all up under the black headlines:

BIRTHPLACE OF WATER SKIIKG—Lake City,
Samuelson Feted at Water Show

Thousands of Lake Citians, area residents, and tourists gathered on the shores of Lake Pepin Sunday to honor the man who has been officially designated as "The Father of Water Skiing."

Ralph Samuelson, a Lake City native now living in Pine Island, was presented with a three-foot trophy certifying the claim to be the first skier, and Lake City to be the birthplace of water skiing.

A full slate of dignitaries and entertainers provided a colorful and thrilling program for the throngs watching from the beach and park. The Prior Lake Ski Club presented their specialty act before a crowd estimated to be made up of 8,000 to 10,000 persons.

Overcast skies and mild temperatures provided perfect weather conditions for viewing the program. There was no sun glare on the water, and predicted showers did not materialize until well after the crowds had dispersed.

One of the spectacular events of the program was the skydiving exhibition by Richard Hoyt, who jumped from a plane and landed on the beach precisely on target, the general area of Samuelson's first water skiing adventure.

The only event on the program which did not come off according to schedule was the flight of the 1908 plane which was to have been flown "by Walter Bullock, retired Northwest Airlines pilot, who towed Samuelson on skis in 1925 behind a flying boat." The plane didn't make, but Bullock did.

The entire program was under the sponsorship of the Lake City Chamber of Commerce.

The respected *Rochester Post-Bulletin*, of the nearby Mayo Clinic city, brought some additional details.

Lake City Graphic

It pointed out that Ralph was now 63 and that he was tempted to ski at the event, but let his three children, Karen, Debbie, and Jon participate instead.

The *Post-Bulletin* stated that the water parade had 25 decorated boats in it, Charlyne Wold riding the first one; and that the jump made by Richard Hoyt was from a height of 10,000 feet, and that as a member of the European Military Parachute Team he had completed 260 jumps. Also, that Ralph was booked solid through the summer and the rest of the year for water ski and boat shows, here and abroad.

The paper was right. The long-forgotten inventor of water skiing had already received an invitation to be guest of honor at the next World Water Ski Championship to be held in Canada.

Clint Ward, Tournament Chairman had invited him. Ralph answered with a wire, "We gave your kind invitation our earliest attention and accept gladly. Canada, here we come."

One editorial, appearing in the *Red Wing Republican* two days after the event at Lake City, was almost prophetic. Said the editor:

> The man who represented the American Water Ski Association at Lake City's festival Sunday had a thoughtful comment to make. "Man," he said, "has a remarkable capacity for exploring and enjoying himself in places far removed from his natural environment."
>
> The evidence was plainly and dramatically visible during Sunday's Lake City program. It showed not only in the stunts and antics while skimming along Lake Pepin's surface on small pieces of wood. There were also the water skiers who soared 50 feet above the water and flew around and around, via kite; and the skydiver who plunged from 8,000 feet and landed miraculously on the scheduled spot right in front of Lake City's bathhouse.
>
> Pure frivolity, you can call all this. But do not scoff. It's this same human drive to explore the unknown, to do the never-done-before, that has yielded all kinds of new knowledge and has greatly improved the physical circumstances of human life.
>
> Water ski founder Ralph Samuelson was a kindred spirit, in his time, of those intrepid souls who have scaled Mount Everest, descended to the ocean depths, and rocketed 'round and 'round our globe in space.
>
> Lake City staged a first-class event Sunday. Seeing these events of derring-do so close at hand leaves us without doubt that man is destined soon to put his footsteps on the moon.

Man did—only 1,125 days later, on July 20, 1969.

The gentleman who represented the American Water Ski Association at the event, and partly inspired the above editorial, was John Osberg, a member of the board of directors, and a resident of White Bear, Minnesota, the same place where Ralph had performed before the Kiwanians, 43 years earlier.

And what of the man who did it first—who had been neglected, laughed at, mocked and teased, called a ham and worse, who had been stared at in Detroit and Florida, who had been hailed as the daredevil of the decade, and then had been completely, absolutely, 100 percent forgotten, until the Fairy Godmother, Margaret Crimmins, and her charioteer, Ben Simons, rediscovered him? What did Ralph Samuelson think of it all—of the new honor, the adulation, the admiring stares, the trophy, the interviews, the photographs, the editorials?

Had his attitude toward life changed? Was he conceited? Puffed up?

He himself commented on his new glory: "June 19, 1966, was perhaps the greatest day of my life, when I was honored as the first water skier in the world.

"But now, more than ever, I realized that this recognition and honor came as the result of a spiritual battle I had been fighting for over a decade.

"My feelings at this time can be summed up in a few words. The events of the day humbled me greatly. It increased my faith to see God's promise come to pass in my life. I thank the Lord for the opportunity of bringing honor and glory to His name.

"After going through the humbling process so many years, I certainly did not get a swelled head.

"But this I admit with delight: I did have an inner joy from the realization that an ordinary person like myself could receive such recognition through the whole world."

As for Margaret Crimmins and Ben Simons, they, of course, "carried out what God had planned and engineered. They were the instruments He used for His purpose. No human being could plan anything as great as this."

And his wife? She took everything in her gentle stride. She hadn't expected Ralph to get this recognition. Now that it had come she felt gratified—and content.

Being a very practical person not given to emotional demonstrations, the hope undoubtedly crossed her mind that this might possibly help out their financial situation.

It didn't, not very much, as time proved.

Hazel remembered all the hours she had been the breadwinner in the family. Now honor was being heaped on Ralph. Nobody bothered much with Hazel. But there were compensations for her. For one thing, Ralph had been vindicated. She felt happy about that.

What no paper mentioned, and what Ralph himself didn't talk much about until later, was the almost mystic feeling he had when once again he stood on the shore of the Lake which had played such an important part in his life—the body of water which, above all else, had shaped his being, his life, his philosophy, his religion.

As he looked out on that Lake, while dignitaries and officials pressed around him, congratulated him, presented him with a gigantic trophy he almost felt as if he should share that big silver cup with the Lake.

"It seemed to me that cloudy afternoon, while the Lake lay quiet and peaceful, almost as it had that day 44 years ago, as if she was smiling at me—or rather winking.

"It was as if we understood each other. She was telling me, 'Well, old boy, did you ever think it would come to this? Oh, never mind thanking me. It was you who conquered me. You weren't afraid of me as so many others, and together we did it. You and me.'

"'And God,' I told the Lake. But then you don't have to tell Nature about God, I guess. It's part of God, as the Lake is part of Him."

Other recognition came to Ralph Samuelson.

For one thing, he was invited to attend the Chicago National Boat Show, guest of Johnson Motors, whose boats he had raced back in affluent times. He received flattering publicity in the Windy City.

As Ralph pointed out in a letter to Hardman, he was also invited to come to the State Office Building in St. Paul, where he was asked by the Director of Publicity and Promotion to represent the state on various occasions, primarily boat shows.

The next year, Ralph returned to the Chicago show for the Taperflex Water Ski Company of California, spent time in their booth, helping to promote the sale of their skis. Compensation? Expenses only.

To earn a living, Ralph Samuelson, slowly becoming a national figure, continued his modest work with the Minnesota Highway Department as just another employee.

The following winter, still basking in the after glow of the glory that had finally decided to shine round about him, he spent time with his loving family.

And then it was time to take full advantage of the invitation to the Tenth World Water Ski Championship, Montreal, Canada, as per Clint Ward's invitation. Ralph was to be the official guest of honor, expenses paid.

All through his first foreign appearance, Ralph Samuelson, as he admitted later, felt like a boy with a new bicycle, a man who wakes up and finds that the good dream he's been having wasn't a dream at all.

Much to his credit be it said, he represented the United States admirably, modestly, behaved like a veteran to whom being a guest of honor at numerous banquets, parades, cocktail parties, receptions, awarding of championship medals were a common occurrence.

Lake City, by the way, did its share for this trip, put a rented car at the disposal of the Samuelsons for the duration.

For a week, it was all activity. In Montreal, and out at the tournament site, Sherbrooke, Ralph was a marked man, with a huge ribbon on his lapel—a golden VIP on a purple background showing a jumping water skier, and the words World Waterski Championship. Championship Mondial du Ski Nautique, Sherbrooke, Aug. 2-Sept 3, 1967.

It was all under the distinguished patronage of His Excellency the Right Honorable Roland Michener, Governor General of Canada.

Publicity followed him and Hazel. Articles appeared in the *Montreal Star*, and the Sherbrooke papers. The official program gave Samuelson a centerspread, with photographs, new and old, and a reprint of Margaret Crimmins' story as it had appeared in *The Water Skier*.

Ralph was especially impressed with the showmanship of the many member nations.

Said Ralph, when he finally got home. "I received a beautiful gold medal with ribbon, as memento of the event. I had the pleasure of meeting and talking with many of the water skiers from all over the world.

"It was all magnificent, dramatic action. Each country had its own separate colored uniforms: the Australians had a beautiful green one with a kangaroo patch; others had stars, leaves, designs of many geometric figures, shields, dragons, even a deer and a rooster as identifying symbols. It certainly made me realize how far skiing had progressed. It was a whole new world, a challenging world.

"I received a book about Japanese water skiing which had many of my pictures in it. They had gotten as far as Japan! The author was the Director of the Japanese Water Ski Association, Masonori Komorimiya. He wanted to be called Komo, which suited me fine. The book, 300 pages, is a how-to manual, published in Japan. The author inscribed it for me: "To Mr. Ralph Samuelson, our most respectable Father of Water Skiing."

"The whole thing was a great joy to me—greater than anything I had ever experienced in my life."

Ralph lived with those memories for months.

He wondered—would the world forget him again?

Or wasn't God through with Ralph Samuelson yet?

50. ANOTHER MIRACLE

Ralph Samuelson would be the last to admit it, but there was a definite letdown in his life after the big events at Lake City and in Canada.

Working at a humdrum job with the humdrum highway department wasn't much of a thrill. Taking care of the chores around the house became a bit of a duty, not a spiritual uplift.

Ralph had received some recognition in Detroit and Florida, but it had been on a small scale, really. Now through the American Water Ski Association he had been fed his first nice bite of national recognition. He liked the taste of it.

He would have been superhuman if all the attention, temporary as it was, had not raised his ego, in spite of his religiously inspired modesty.

Just as he had been forgotten after 1928, when his broken back made skiing impossible, so now the new peak of publicity leveled off, too—in a plain, if not another valley.

Oh, true, he had some flattering requests for autographs, some fan letters, various business concerns, mostly manufacturers of boats, asked him to endorse their products, but, on the whole, life became unexciting again.

It was shortly after his Lake City experience that I first met Ralph Samuelson.

I had missed that 1966 celebration. As an educational director of an Institute of Learning in Long Beach, I couldn't arrange my vacation in Lake City, my wife's hometown, and our annual Mecca since 1939.

We arrived in Minnesota from California after June 20. All I heard when I got to Lake City was "Water Ski Festival. Oh, it was great!" A few days later, I drove over to Pine Island and had a pleasant interview with Ralph and his gracious wife Hazel.

I was hoping to do an article, perhaps a book, on Ralph.

I found a tall, stalwart, rugged Swede, with penetrating blue eyes, a curving nose, his tawny hair still combed back and parted in the middle, as the pictures had portrayed him when he first got on top of Lake Pepin. The wrinkles of his 63 years were so evenly and gently distributed, he looked younger than he was.

His smile was friendly, but guarded; his speech dignified and clipped. He didn't waste words, spoken in a slightly husky voice.

We had a long discussion. In the immaculately clean, modern, but certainly not pretentious home, I got the impression that Ralph Samuelson didn't want anybody to write a book about him. The thought intruded; perhaps he wanted to do it himself?

That was dispelled by his last words: "If I'm ever ready to have a book done about me, you'll be the first to know."

Was it some form of modesty that held him back at that time? Or some inner voice? Did he feel God hadn't given him the proper sign?

Even then, I realized how intimately Ralph Samuelson lived with his personal God.

His shelf contained religious books and magazines. His favorite seemed to be the Golden Book of Oswald Chambers, *My Utmost for His Highest*, a volume of daily meditations. I remembered that Chambers was a great evangelistic mystic and of noble spiritual stature.

Even at that meeting Ralph spoke of God as if he talked with Him freely and often.

Although I didn't hear the details of how he lay out under the evening sky and felt the need of God, and heard God answer, he used such expressions as "new birth," "God has chosen me for a great purpose." "It's not what you know but what you are that counts before God." "Modern religion does not mean a thing. Most people who go to church didn't experience a new birth at all."

I left our interview and forgot about Ralph Samuelson, as so many others had.

Apparently God didn't forget.

Eventually it was time for Him to test Ralph Samuelson again. At least that's what Ralph thought.

"I became ill. Sick. Very sick. But in my childlike faith I said to myself, 'You'll get over it'. But I discovered that God doesn't always heal through miracles, nice as that would be. We have no right to tell God how to heal us. He may do it through a good doctor, or he may choose to do it through prayer."

Ralph, listening to his childlike faith, didn't go to a doctor in time. When he finally consulted a local physician. His trouble was diagnosed as uremic poisoning. He was put on antibiotics.

He didn't improve, lost 40 pounds, until he was too weak to walk.

His doctor finally gave up, hustled his patient over to nearby Rochester.

His case was diagnosed again: prostate gland surgery was necessary—immediately.

And now came another miracle, so Ralph believes. He had been prepared for surgery, was quietly waiting to go up to the operating room, when he felt a large lump on his lower abdomen. Ralph knew he had a small hernia, but no doctor had even detected it.

Ralph called the nurse, the nurse called the doctor, the doctor called Ralph an uncomplimentary name and growled, "What did you do to bring this on? This is a strangling type of hernia!"

"I've just been lying here, Doc," objected Ralph. "Waiting to go up to surgery. Haven't even been out of bed, thanks to these, these handy bedpans."

"Call the specialist," the physician told the nurse.

The specialist came. "Get this man the hell out of here up to surgery before this thing strangles his intestines," the man commanded.

Ralph had two operations simultaneously.

After a day or so, the hernia specialist gave his opinion: "You were mighty lucky this thing happened where and when it did. Anywhere else, and you probably wouldn't have made it at all. Patients like you respond to medication infinitely better than others. Prayers help a patient to heal much quicker it seems. You'll be out sooner than any patient I've ever had."

"Because a Christian has no fear to overcome," explained Ralph. "He can concentrate all his faith on recovery."

Ralph did recover in record time.

Home again, he wondered if his big, red book of clippings of the 1966 water ski celebration at Lake City, and the subsequent events in Canada were as far as he'd ever go.

Not that he was resentful. He had had at least a taste of glory. More and more he was steeping himself in religious thoughts, trying to be a good adviser and friend to his three children. He held his vanity strictly in check.

Karen, a nurse, had gotten married, in the fall of 1969, and was living in Minneapolis. The other two children came home from college whenever possible. Hazel was still teaching.

Then, after life had settled into a grove of sorts, Ralph read a preliminary report in the *Lake City Graphic.*

Something really big was coming up, and he would play an important part in it.

History was marching on, and taking Ralph Samuelson along!

{8}

Section

51. THE TOWN, 50 YEARS LATER

As far back as 1968, water ski devotees had a gleam in their eyes. Their golden anniversary was coming up!

If, as the American Water Ski Association had proclaimed, water skiing was invented—evolved from other water activities might be a better way of saying it, according to Thomas Hardman—in 1922, then 1972 was it!

Had Fred Waller been given the credit, water skiers would have been forced to wait until 1975. Had the honor been given to Don Ibsen, they would have postponed the event until 1978. Had it been invented in France, nobody here would have bothered, probably.

Later, in a beautiful issue of *The Water Skier*, a 62-page extra, with a golden cover displaying a big golden 50 on a blue background, and the numbers 1922-1972 overcrossed skis, the president of the American Water Ski Association at the time, Stillman A. Bell, summed it up in a short editorial:

To have endured 50 years of growing pains, technical advances and world-wide involvement is certainly a tribute to our sport of water skiing—a Golden Anniversary worth celebrating at our Nationals in Seattle, August 17, 18, 19, 20.

From Ralph Samuelson's ride 50 years ago on those two long, homemade skis, to Wayne Grimditch's 169-foot jump in the recent Masters is indeed a long step in progress. Our progress has brought us to the threshold of the Olympics. This year in September, water skiing for the first time ever will be involved in the Olympics as a demonstration sport.

Who first planted the seed in the minds of Lake City officials that it was up to them to tie in with the great event nobody seems to remember. Perhaps Samuelson did it at a meeting with the Chamber of Commerce. Ben Simons, always on his toes when it came to any important event to promote the harbor, may have needled officials.

Be that as it may—if God wanted to heap another honor on the head of His trusting servant, Ralph Samuelson, He got the help He needed.

I was doing a historic novel set in the famous so-called Half-breed Tract, that slice of land running from Red Wing along the Mississippi River and Lake Pepin, down to the mouth of the Buffalo River, south of Lake City—including all of that city.

While doing research on the whole area, I came across the information that the charter of incorporation of Ralph Samuelson's hometown had been signed and sealed at St. Paul in February of 1872.

If anybody else in town was aware of that when I met with a special committee, the Retail Group of the Chamber of Commerce, at their headquarters on South Lakeshore Drive in June of 1969, they kept it very quiet.

The committee, under the chairmanship of Hollace Abraham, prominent owner of a well-stocked hardware store, was interested in making plans for some sort of celebration of the 50th water ski anniversary—nothing else.

Abraham, always eager to boost Lake Pepin as a powerful attraction for fishermen, hoped the anniversary celebration would
make the country more aware of the Lake.

He flattered me by inviting me to attend a planning luncheon.
I had worked with radio, television, newspapers for many years,
was a member of the Overseas Press Club, the Association of Radio and Television News Analysts, and the Public Relations Society of America. So, after a pleasant luncheon, we talked about
the anniversary.

The conversation went something like this, between me and
some of the members, among them Herb Hinck, Dean Sperling,
Cliff Sogla, Ray Cashman, Harley Eggenberger, Ray Jones, Pat
Wise, Graham Illingsworth, and Shelly Peterson.

None of them had signed that Chamber of Commerce affidavit to the American Water Ski Association nearly four years
before, but all were vitally interested in their town.

Somewhere along the line I believe I said, "Why don't you make it
bigger than just an event for the 50th anniversary of water skiing."

Said somebody: "What's the matter, don't you think the 50th
anniversary of water skiing is important?"

"Sure it's important," said I.

"But you're not a water skier, are you?"

"Frankly, no."

"That's why."

"I'm not saying water skiing isn't important. But plan bigger," said I.

"You said that."

"Did you know, for instance, that the same year which is the
50th anniversary of water skiing, is also the 100th anniversary of
the incorporation of your city?"

There was silence.

"How'd you know that?" asked somebody finally.

"It's in the records. At your library. At the State House. The charter of Lake City was signed in February 1872. You'll be 100 years old in 1972. What a big thing it would be if you'd celebrate both events at the same time. You'd really have something! Give the whole town a reason to participate, not only those interested in water skiing. You'll have a double entry of such proportions that you'll really get attention, not only in Wabasha County, but the state, the whole nation."

More silence.

The chairman broke it. "This sure puts a different face on the whole thing. This could be really big."

It turned out to be just that—big!

What followed in the next few years is too complicated to narrate in detail—and primarily of local interest.

But the businessmen of Lake City were sharp boys. They kept in touch with the world.

They caught fire.

Slowly at first, then with more determination, they got going, much to the glory of Lake City, Birthplace of Water Skiing, and more to the glory of Ralph Samuelson, Father of Water Skiing.

Never underestimate an American community effort once the spirit gets them a movin'.

Before I left that fall to return to California, the *Lake City Graphic*, under the guidance of its publisher, Larry Oberg, and its editor, Esther Oberg, started to boost plans for the combination 50th and 100th anniversary.

Cleverly they printed teasers that aroused people's curiosity, piqued them into thinking—and remembering.

Cliff Sogla, chairman of the general chamber, appointed a Centennial Committee. That winter the Chamber wrote me for suggestions. I outlined a plan.

I suggested not one short event, but year-round activities. One month the schools were to take over, put on a historical pageant reviewing the history of the town; another month the women's organizations would plan centennial events, a fashion show, displays, spelling bees—what not. The Chamber would do something one month; the service clubs, the churches, the Legion, the VFW, the Country Club, all would participate somehow.

Every month throughout the year there would be something.

And one peaked high spot in summer would be the special water ski anniversary event. It should be scheduled for Sunday, July 2, the exact 50th anniversary by month and day of Samuelson's victory.

That would be the day for a big combination parade. The whole state, the American Water Ski Association and various ski groups would participate.

The following summer, I gave a talk before the Kiwanis Club in Lake City, urging them to speed up their tempo even more. Some of the committees were dragging their feet.

As the anniversary year approached, things got into high gear. Ideas came rolling in. Plans were made for a parade, a water show, competitions like giving prizes to the man who could raise the most successful Centennial placards and buttons were designed.

A dozen committees planned for special effects in decoration, display of utensils of the past century in store windows, collections of old photographs to be printed in the *Graphic*; and a centennial booklet was proposed. A hundred different ideas were submitted and discussed; many were adopted.

It became a community effort such as the town had never seen!

Said the *Graphic* in a special pre-anniversary edition:

> A combined Centennial and Water Skiing Celebration of the magnitude of the one expected to take place here during the first week in July, is not arranged overnight.
>
> Many local committees have worked diligently to arrange the outstanding series of events which are expected to draw thousands of visitors to Lake City, particularly on July 2, when the big parade and water show are scheduled.

"It's been fun," said Hans Tauchnitz, general chairman, who adds ruefully, "but it's a lot of work!"

In addition to the chairman the Centennial Committee included Emery Zillgitt, Dean Sperling, Kenneth Garbisch, Hollace Abraham, Don Karow, Jaycee President, Dan Gathje, Ray Cashman, Ray Tiedemann, Dave McCormick, and Linda Farrington, Linda Watson, Chamber of Commerce Secretary, has served as secretary of the group. Herb Hinck, Chamber of Commerce president is Centennial Committee treasurer.

Numerous assistants have worked with the committee heads to help make the Centennial a success, Jerry Weinman, and Jim Siewert are co-chairmen of the Centennial Parade, which is sponsored by the Jaycees. Other committee members include Kenneth Willers, Eugene Durand, Dick Sitta, Dan Gathje, Keith Willers, Bob Plote, Lenny Weber, Dave Moses, Phil Gartner, and Steve Ritzenthaler

Ray Cashman has been in charge of Centennial button sales, and Ray Tiedemann of Centennial emblem sales. Hollace Abraham and Don Karow have handled Brothers of the Brush (beards, button sales, and issuance of shaving permits). Mrs. Glen Dwelle has been in charge of Sisters of the Swish buttons, Don Kriett is president of the Brothers of the Brush organization.

A Centennial booklet is being planned under the direction of Chairman Lester Howatt, and will be published at a later date,

Tom Kennedy, Dean Sperling and Pat Wise comprise the Fireworks Committee.

Kenneth Garbisch was chairman of the Historical Slide Program at Lincoln High School last winter, working in cooperation with the Lake City division of the Wabasha County Historical Society, and the Lake City Teachers Association.

Hiawathaland Executive Secretary Doyle Sorenson has ably assisted the Centennial Committee in many ways.

In addition to individuals, many local organizations have assisted in various ways to make the celebration a success. The Wabasha County Historical Society, the Garden clubs, and others have worked with the committee.

The Graphic would like to give credit to everyone who has helped to arrange Centennial or Water Skiing events to date. If your name has inadvertently been omitted, please call so that we can give public recognition to your work which may have helped to make past Centennial events a success or is helping to prepare for the spectacular upcoming weekend celebration.

By the time this article appeared, Lake City was half-way through its centennial year celebrations, and Ralph Samuelson had been guest of honor at almost every one of them.

The historical pageant with special period music, given by the high school before two overflow audiences, had been a big success. The Woman's Club had put on special programs of historical significance with a gala fashion show featuring dresses of the previous century; the garden clubs had arranged award-winning displays.

Plans were being made for the second half of the year, which was to end with a joyous New Year's Eve party in which three or four organizations would sponsor simultaneous centennial shindigs. Lake City would enter its second century in high spirits—praising the name of Ralph Samuelson, their most famous Centennial character.

Now the big day was approaching—July 2, 1972—the Golden Anniversary of the first successful attempt of a human being to slide on top of water.

Not just any water, Lake City's own Lake Pepin. And the hero of the occasion would be the man who did it—Ralph Samuelson.

He would be there, in person!

52. THE DAY, 50 YEARS LATER

July 2, 1972, dawned red in the sky beyond Lake Pepin. A cool, fragrant, green and gold Minnesota summer day was coming up.

Who is to deny that the Spirit of the Lake was aware it was the 50th anniversary of a day when she had carried on her unstable, liquid surface the gargantuan skis of a stubborn young

Swede? She had carried many since, but his were the first. He had refused to give up until he had emerged out of her, to glide on top of her waves.

No need to try and capture the excitement of that day, as the celebrities arrived; the cars from a dozen states began to clutter every street in Lake City, until they were parked 25 blocks from the center of town.

Tension built up at the Press Center, very near the identical spot where Ralph Samuelson's father once ran his grocery store, in the banquet room of the Embassy Bar on Center Street.

There the reporters were presented with press badges, press kits, fact sheets, pictures of Ralph Samuelson, then and now.

And they were there in surprising number, UPI, AP, Chicago Tribune, St. Louis and Milwaukee papers, all the dailies and weeklies of adjoining counties and the Twin Cities—reporters, columnists, special sports writers—a total of 57, plus five more recording for radio, and four taping and filming for TV.

The most nervous activity sprouted around the small, cut-off semicircle south of town, near the government pier, where a newly erected stone cairn, already bearing the special bronze plaque donated by the Minnesota Historical Society, was still covered, guarded by Boy Scouts.

Still farther south, on Lakeshore Drive, floats, bands, horses, fire engines, antique cars, clowns, decorated limousines, and more floats jockeyed for their designated positions, until there were 186 units—20 percent more than had been anticipated—an unprecedented number of participants for a small town of less than 4,000 population.

Along the parade route, carefully announced in advance, spectators were settling down on blankets, on the grass, on the curbs. The cries of hucksters, the antics of the Brothers of the Brush, no two beards alike, the marching of the Sisters of the Swish in their beautiful, gay, 19th Century gowns and hats, formed a colorful background.

The Water Ski Anniversary reached its climax punctually at 12:30. Somebody had suggested it be scheduled at 4:11 p.m. the exact minute when "Sammy did it;" but 12:30 was close enough to being exactly 50 years later.

Again it was Sunday, as it had been then.

And again Ralph was the center of attraction, more so, even— a tall, rugged Swede, one day short of his 69th birthday, attired in a natty Commodore uniform, a blue, double-breasted blazer with silver buttons, white pants and white tie, a blue shirt, white shoes, and a skipper's cap, complete with the customary scrambled eggs on the visor.

Ralph's blazer really blazed with a red, white and blue circular patch, the U.S. shield in the center, the words "Father of Water Skiing" above, "R. Samuelson" below.

In front of the cairn a huge bed of blooming, crimson Cana lilies, vari-colored petunias, and gay phlox may have reminded Ralph of his days with Eric Wilson of the nursery, dead 40 years.

Ralph was driven to the dedication winner's circle in an open car. Dignitaries followed: Robert Wheeler, now Assistant Director of the Minnesota Historical Society, the same man who had helped Ralph find his pictures and old newspapers nearly 10 years ago; U.S. Congressman Albert H. Quie; Lake City's Mayor, Wilmer (Tony) Strickland; Centennial Committee Chairman, Hans Tauchnitz; Miss Minnesota, Linda Hagan; Herbert Hinck, Chamber President; Harbormaster Ben Simons; and Parade Grand Marshall Barry Zevan, a Twin City TV personality.

Legislators were there: State Senator Roger Laufenberger and Senator George Conzemius; State Representatives Vic Schultz and Richard Lemke, from Red Wing, the birthplace of organized snow ski jumping, came Dale Mehrkens, representing his town's Chamber of Commerce,

Lake City Graphic

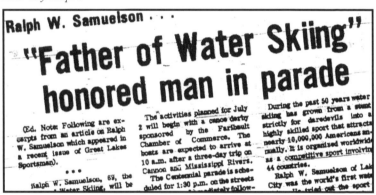

Lake City Graphic

The master of ceremonies, Emery Zillgitt, official of the Lake City Savings and Loan Association, called the meeting to order.

Reporters, photographers and TV writers, cameramen, columnists, all crowded closer as Samuelson took his place by the stone altar, still covered with its scarlet velvet blanket, his name in golden letters.

The mayor welcomed everybody, the guests of honor were introduced, beginning with "the man who started all this, the

Father of Water Skiing himself, Ralph Samuelson."

The master of ceremonies called on Robert Wheeler, who made a short, comment:

> Thank you, Mr. Chairman, the Honorable Albert H. Quie, distinguished guests. A few years ago an unassuming, self-effacing man called on the Minnesota Historical Society, and told me the incredible story of how in 1922 he had strapped a couple of pine boards to his feet and skied along the surface of Lake Pepin behind a motor boat; and later at the speed of 80 miles an hour behind a seaplane.
>
> On that July day in 1922, Ralph Samuelson had little idea of the significance of this achievement; nor did he know that half a century later the Minnesota Historical Society would be erecting a plaque commemorating an event which has already been recorded in the annals of sports history.
>
> On behalf of the Minnesota Historical Society we are pleased and honored to present this plaque to Lake City. Thank you.

Together Ralph Samuelson and Congressman Quie lifted the heavy cover from the plaque. Photographers took close-ups. Everybody applauded.

At the top of the plaque, Ralph Samuelson is skiing behind a motor boat; in the lower right-hand corner are the seal of the Society with its pioneer figures, and the words, "Instituted 1849."

The text is in boldly raised bronze letters:

HISTORIC LAKE PEPIN BIRTHPLACE OF WATER SKIING
"I decided that if you could ski on snow, you could ski on water." In 1922, after first trying barrel staves, then snow ski, eighteen year old Ralph W. Samuelson succeeded in waterskiing on eight foot long pine boards, steamed in boiling water to curve the tips. During the next fifteen years, Samuelson put on one-man waterskiing exhibitions, donating most of the admission charges to Lake City for the purchase of harbor and parkland. Because of Samuelson's pioneering efforts in this popular sport, the American Water Ski Association in 1966 officially

recognized Lake City as the birthplace of waterskiing.
Erected by the Minnesota Historical Society

The master of ceremonies introduced other celebrities, including Ben Simons, then called on Congressman Quie, who made the dedication address. Said the Congressman, speaking without notes:

> Thank you, Emery and friends. It is certainly a great honor to be here as we dedicate the plaque in commemoration of the 50 years since water skiing began.
>
> As you read the words on that plaque, "I decided that if you could ski on snow, you could ski on water," and as you look out over this lake and see water skiers any time, you have to recognize that 50 years ago nobody did that it took a particularly different kind of man, a person who had special attributes to begin it.
>
> One of these attributes, it seems to me, is faith in one's self. And Ralph Samuelson had that when he believed that if you could ski on snow he could ski on water as well.
>
> He had that faith back in 1922, and again in 1925 when he skied behind an airplane, hanging on to that ring at the end of a long sash, knowing that if he'd fall, he'd be in trouble.
>
> He did fall, but as he told me, he skidded along on his belly, too fast, even, to sink into the water. Have you ever had the experience of burning your backside on water?
>
> That's what Ralph Samuelson did when he took that kind of speed run. And he followed through, in a kind of daredevil way, when he went to Florida, where apparently some people saw him and took the idea to the French Riviera. That's why some Frenchmen think they started water skiing.
>
> But in 1966 it was indisputably recognized that Ralph Samuelson began water skiing with his daring feat.
>
> But what was more important, I think, was the courage of the man and his faith he had in himself. He believed he could do what nobody had done before, and he did it.
>
> You know, you can climb a mountain and think you're the only one who ever climbed it. Then, on top, when you reach it, you find

an empty pop can, and you know somebody was there before you.

But there was no pop can at the end of Ralph Samuelson's accomplishment. It was an absolute first with him.

He didn't know what would happen to him, especially at high speeds behind an airplane.

I think Lake City is really fortunate to have it all happen here. Oh, what this can mean to your community.

But there is something more about Ralph Samuelson about which I'd like to make a short comment.

It's this. Ralph didn't only have faith in himself, as you can see today when you look at him, 50 years later. He had faith in God.

It's Sunday. And as we dedicate this plaque, we should turn our minds to that. Ralph Samuelson really believed in God. He knows that that is happening to him is not of his own doing. He knows now that he was playing a part in the purpose of the Lord here on earth. I think that is his real strength.

You know, there were countless persons in history whom you would like to interrogate, and ask, "How did it happen? How did you do it?" But they've passed on, and can't tell us.

But here—today—it's different. It's tremendous that we can honor Ralph on this, the 50th anniversary of water skiing, and have him right here with us! We can ask him questions: What was it like? How did it feel? And he's here to tell us.

What a great thing it would be, Ralph, if we could ask you questions for many years to come—let's say, at least 50. You've got to make it until you're 100.

There's something grand about our heritage, and our country. We are a country that believes in itself, has courage to try something new.

All around us we see the work of Americans who have proved they are not afraid to do this.

We do it with faith in God. That faith is written in the greatest document of our government; it is written in our edifices, in our communities.

This faith is personified in our Ralph Samuelson!

It is a great pleasure to be with you, as we share this day with a tremendously great American.

Thank you!

The applause—long, loud, sincere—echoed across the Lake. Ralph Samuelson bowed his head, so his family, nearby, wouldn't see the tears trickling down his slightly wrinkled, tanned cheeks, glowing with pride and humility "at the wonder of it all!"

The group slowly dispersed. As many as could get near shook Ralph's hand.

Then it was time for the parade—another highlight in Ralph Samuelson's life, for he rode on the Lake City Centennial float as the guest of honor, a giant centennial sign as background, flanked by three bikini-clad beauties. The side of the float proclaimed him "Father of Water Skiing."

The late Tony Strickland, gentle and efficient mayor of the town, and his wife, rode in the well-preserved and polished antique 1937 Mercedes, which I had succeeded in getting out of Nazi Germany when Hitler's authorities closed the American Colony School in Berlin.

The parade took four full hours to pass the judges' stand. It revealed to a slightly stunned audience of some 40,000, 10 times Lake City's regular population, that human beings can think up when they make up their minds.

The floats ranged from a huge, pink birthday cake with 100 electric candles, to a figure doing a simulated ski jump from a toed of red flowers. One float was built like a motorboat pulling a skier. One resembled Bullock's old seaplane.

The parade had clanging fire engines, a dozen high school bands in their elaborate uniforms, valuable classic cars, several drum corps, bugle corps, drill teams, clowns, horses, and floats, floats, floats.

Reporters like Big John Husar of the *Chicago Tribune*, Myron Holtzman of the *St. Louis Globe-Democrat*, Henry Fisher of the *Red Wing Republican-Eagle*, Jim Johnson of the *Winona Daily News*, Lynda McDonnel of the *Rochester Post-Bulletin*, reporters from the Twin Cities, all the following week wrote glowingly that at long last Ralph Samuelson was really receiving the honors long overdue.

The only celebrity not present was Margaret Crimmins, unable to get away from duties with the *Washington Post.*

And Samuelson?

After it was all over, wonderment was written more plainly than ever on his rugged features. Said he: "Little did I dream when I was a child on this beautiful Lake, that they would be honoring me by its shore, calling me a living legend, a child of Destiny, Lake City's God-given asset and a dozen other flattering names."

After a delay caused by a sudden Minnesota July shower, the water ski exhibition by the White Bear Water Ski Club, with fantastic, professional demonstrations, proved how fantastically far water skiing had dared to progress in 50 years.

"It was all too wonderful," Ralph summed it up. "But after all, as Congressman Quie pointed out, I didn't do it. God did it—through me!

"The beautiful plaque will stand there to remind future generations of what God has wrought."

"But the red velvet cover I took home. Hazel asked me if I wanted to be buried in it. Not a bad idea! But, not yet. Life is getting to be too interesting!"

53. THE POSTSCRIPT

Ralph Samuelson turned 69 the day after the anniversary parade in which his name was linked with that of a 100-year-old city, and a Lake that God had put there millions of years ago.

"To me that Lake suddenly looked even more glamorous," said Ralph some weeks after the historic event. "It was as if she was talking to me again, as she had back in 1966, telling me, 'I told you, someday you'd realize what we accomplished. Of course to me this is just another milestone to be added to my other background as the pathway of the ages for explorers, missionaries, soldiers, speculators, emigrants, modern businessmen.

'To me being the Birthplace of Water Skiing is just one more notch on the totem pole of History; just one more plaque added to the ones already decorating my shore. But, come to think of it, it is a very important one, to be sure.

'The missionaries and the explorers are gone; the old forts along my banks are only historic markers now. But your plaque is different. It's got the interest of the new, sport-minded generation. I've got a feeling that long after they have forgotten Father Hennepin and Nicolas Perrot and Josiah Snelling and Zebulon Pike, the growing number of water skiers will remember you, Ralph Samuelson.'

"Yes sir, that's what the Lake said. And to me it was sweet talk. Not that it made me arrogant. It was as if partners were talking, each giving the other the bigger share of credit."

Whatever happened between Lake Pepin and Ralph Samuelson was private. What happened to the man very soon after the unveiling of his plaque was very public.

He began his public appearances as a personage, a symbol, in Seattle, which had once claimed to be the Birthplace of Water Skiing. That city invited him and Hazel to attend the Golden Anniversary National Water Ski Championship, August 17 to 20 of that same year.

In his usual cryptic, laconic manner Ralph said about it, "In the month of August I was honored in Seattle, Washington."

Honored, indeed.

At first some of Seattle's sports writers were a bit touchy about the new Father of Water Skiing.

When Ralph had come to public attention back in 1966, Byron Fish, an important sports correspondent for the *Seattle Times*, commented on the entire competition and couldn't resist to point out, as he had done several times before that, Seattle had its own claim to water ski fame in its native son Don Ibsen.

But now, Fish yielded to Samuelson's seniority, pointed out, however, that nobody could claim any greater seniority at sticking with the sport than Don Ibsen, who could keep on skiing, while Samuelson, because of his bad back, had to give it up.

Now that Samuelson was actually in Seattle, special guest of officials of the 1972 tournament, and the *Times* gave him excellent coverage, with headlines and photos.

Ralph watched the boys' and men's slaloms, the girls' and women's slaloms, the kite skiing—all the rest, for four days, until the winners were selected and announced.

He took tours, smiled, gratefully when he was recognized, thanks to the official 42-page program, which featured his pictures.

Reminiscing about that Seattle victory tour, Samuelson said, "Hazel and I stayed in one of the large hotels, close to the tournament site. I had the pleasure of finally meeting one of the early pioneers of water skiing, Don Ibsen.

My wife and I had more time there to see sights. We also had breakfast on top of the big space needle, which we enjoyed very much. We stayed about a week in Seattle, and I attended the tournament every day and met many wonderful young people, most of whom I had never seen before.

"Then came the victory banquet, held at the end of the tournament. It was at Tillicum Village, Blake Island, Marine State Park, out in Puget Sound. I had the pleasure of passing out awards to the winners of the tournament. To me that was a great thrill."

Then the zenith of the entire occasion. After the banquet the Board of Directors of the American Water Ski Association had a special meeting, and presented Ralph Samuelson with a Resolution which everafter hung, appropriately framed, in the best room of his home in Pine Island. The scroll, beautifully illuminated in red and gold, reads:

Whereas water skiing is a dynamic sport—the world's fastest growing all-family and competitive sport; and

Whereas water skiing promotes the health, welfare, and vitality of people of all ages: and

Whereas RALPH SAMUELSON had the pioneering spirit, inventiveness and genius to "put it all together" on Lake Pepin at Lake City, in the State of Minnesota in July 1922; and

Whereas it has been 50 years since RALPH SAMUELSON first began this grand adventure we know now as water skiing; and

Whereas many people have benefited greatly from Ralph Samuelson's humble, yet determined beginnings:

Now, therefore, be it resolved that the Board of Directors of the American Water Ski Association, duly assembled this 19th day of August, 1972, at Seattle, Washington, do hereby congratulate, commemorate, laud, honor and respect

***** RALPH SAMUELSON *****

Be it further resolved, that special recognition be given RALPH SAMUELSON this 50th anniversary year by all who recognize and enjoy the sport of water skiing; and

Be it further resolved that this Board does hereby confirm Ralph Samuelson's life membership in the American Water Ski Association; and

Be it further resolved, that membership in the Water Ski Hall of Fame be conferred upon RALPH SAMUELSON; and

Be it further resolved that copies of this resolution be sent to *The Water Skier*, the news media, and the general membership of the American Water Ski Association in recognition of Ralph Samuelson's initial and ongoing contributions to the sport of water skiing.

Passed unanimously

American Water Ski Association

Board of Directors

So there it was: the Hall of Fame. He would be No. 1 in it, once it was finished near Orlando, Florida.

Before he went to Seattle, Ralph had already been interviewed on tape for that "Years to Youth," WCCO-TV, Twin Cities program, by the Robbinsdale Junior High School students. That program, mentioned earlier, was aired in prime evening time, Sept. 28, 1972.

Previous to that, on August 16, Ralph was interviewed, for the CBS television show "You Asked for It" by Jack Smith, at Bald Eagle Lake, Minnesota.

That program began with long shots of daring water skiers, performing tricks, with voice-over narration by the athletic-looking Jack Smith:

> Believe me, that's fun; and if you don't want to take my word for it, you can ask any of the more than 10,000,000 who are enjoying water skiing this year. And water skiing isn't just limited to the United States. It's organized world wide. It's a competitive sport involving 44 countries, and has become part of the Summer Olympics.
>
> It was his love of the sport that made us curious about the history of water skiing when David Dexter, college student of Beverly Hills, California, wrote:
>
> "When I received a new pair of water skis as a birthday gift, the thought occurred to me that they must be quite different from the first pair ever invented. If any of these primitive skis are preserved, could you find and show them to me?"
>
> Mr. Dexter, we traveled all the way to the small town of Pine Island, Minnesota, to find the original water skis, but it was worth it, because we also found the man who invented them: Mr. Ralph Samuelson. Mr. Samuelson, could you tell us something about these skis?

Ralph did, reviewing how he got the idea of skiing on water, how he tried barrel staves, how he made his first skis while the camera zoomed in on the historic boards—telling that they cost him $1 each, while modern skis were more than $100 a pair, but were basically the same as his originals—and as many more details as time allowed.

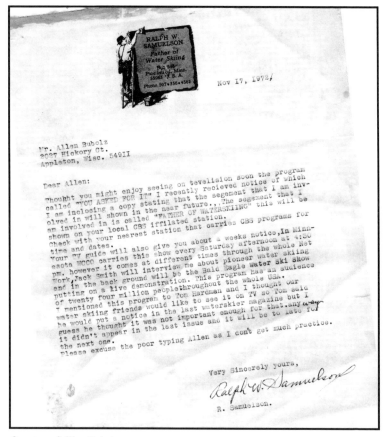

Courtesy of Allen Bubolz

Ralph ended the interview, which the producer claimed had a viewing audience of some 21,000,000, by saying, "I never had any fear. The only fear I had was of losing my bathing suit. It was made of cotton and would stretch and sag. Luckily, I never quite lost it."

One other national honor had come to Ralph in advance of the Seattle event: the National Geographic Society had brought out a book, *The Mighty Mississippi* an account by Bern Keating, with hundreds of photographs by James M. Stanfield.

When Keating got as far as Lake City and Lake Pepin, after beginning his pictorial journey at Lake Itasca, the acknowledged source of the Mississippi, he interviewed Samuelson, and said of him:

> There I met the world's first water skier, Ralph Samuelson, a powerfully-built man. When I shook hands, I could easily believe from his grip that he had been able in 1922 to ride on the world's first water skis despite their enormous drag and slow speed of the boat.

Naturally, Ralph was proud of that mention in a book, which relates the history of the Father of Waters, on which he became the Father of Water Skiing.

Ralph Samuelson was always good copy.

More was to come. In 1973, the Minnesota State Department of Economic Development elected him to be their Good Will Ambassador and sent him to boat shows in Chicago and other large cities, reinforced with press agents, who arranged radio and television appearances, interviews with the press, and got him invitations to banquets where he was often the guest of honor.

The State prepared a fine press kit, an eight-page news release, with fact sheet, pictures, excellent reproductions of old historic ones, many new photos.

Wherever he represented Minnesota and the national sport of water skiing, Ralph did it with dignity, modesty, and always with that sense of wonderment Hardman found so obviously charming in the Father of Water Skiing, as if he were indeed a father who had sired a genius and has to ask himself every time he sees his off spring, "Did I really do that?"

More and more people are thankful that he really did.

The honors go on. Ralph continued to be invited to attend uncounted events, appear as master of ceremonies at parades, not only in Minnesota, but neighboring states, was asked for his autograph a thousand times. He spent summers at a Lake giving ski lessons. Boat companies provided him with boats if he endorsed them, something he did only after he was convinced that he could do it honestly.

All of which did not make him rich. He was not any more commercial minded than he was back in 1922.

He was pleased when he became the subject of a special postage stamp, a blue and green collector's item today.

Clarence Zillgitt, former postmaster of Lake City, one of the signers of the 1965 Chamber affidavit, brought it to my attention.

Davaar Island, issued a special 20 pence stamp, with an aerial photo of Lake City, showing the point and the exact spot where Ralph invented water skiing, and including the area where his plaque now stands. It carries the inscription: "Lake City, Birthplace of Water Skiing, 1922."

Davaar also issued a 5 pence stamp, showing a skier doing a slalom. True, Davaar isn't big. What and where is it? A report of the Stamp Trade Standing Committee, under "British Private Local Issues" states: "DAVAAR, An island at the mouth of the Campbeltown Loch in Argyllshire with a lighthouse on the north-east side. Permanent population of six. Regularly visited by the public from the mainland to view famous cave painting of Christ. Mail is conveyed by boatman privately hired by the occupiers, weekly, weather permitting."

It is not known at this time whether all six citizens of Davaar were water skiers. Most likely. Campbeltown Loch in Argyllshire sounds like a most suitable place for the sport, which has penetrated every corner of the world where there is water.

And little did Ralph Samuelson, the teetotaler anticipate that he would also become the cause of a special label on special whisky, gin and vodka bottles, dispensed by the same Bob Fick, owner of the C & G Liquor Store, Lake City, who was interested enough in Samuelson to write an essay about him, parts of which we have quoted:

"The label designates Lake City as 'The Birthplace of Water

Skiing'. The Harbor House, one of Lake City's most prominent bars and restaurants, gathering place for service clubs, home town folks, and touring visitors, helps distribute the C & G labels—the "Water-ski" liquor…without the water. The Harbor House is owned and op-erated by Mr. and Mrs. Leonard Simons, brother and sister-in-law of Ben Simons, who helped so much to make it all come true.

Some celebrities feel they've arrived when their face or name finally appears on matchbooks. Visitors to Lake City can pick up a matchbook at any time, carrying the text "The Birthplace of Water Skiing, 1922, Lake City, Minn."

Visitors coming to town will also see bright banners at all entrances, designating it to be "The Birthplace of Water Skiing." And, those who continue north along the River to St. Paul can visit the famous skis that hung in Ben Simons boathouse. They are no on display at Minnesota Historical Society museum.

Ralph enjoyed lasting recognitions in the months before his death of cancer in 1977. Most presigiously, Ralph was the guest of honor when the Water Ski Hall of Fame museum was officially dedicated in 1977 in Florida.

Most personally, Ralph was on the shores of his sacred Lake Pepin when Lake City and the State of Minnesota unveiled a huge stylized bronze monument—shaped like the waves he jumped in his youth—in September of 1976 to honor the Father of Water Skiing. It still gleams in the very cove where Samuelson first rose from the waters of Lake Pepin. Engraved upon it are Tom Hard-man's words:

> "If we had a way of foreordaining these things, organized wa-ter skiing couldn't have picked a finer 'father' than Ralph Samuelson. He has been a real asset in promoting the sport since his 'discovery' a dozen years ago, largely because of his modesty and his genuine wonderment at what he started quite innocently back in 1922."

Ralph insisted that all of his accolades, be they inscriptions on whisky bottles, banners, or bronze waves, could not have happened if God had not planned it that way.

Neither, Ralph said, would this book have happened. Another man, Don Karow, former superintendent of schools, had been after Ralph for years to write it all down before he forgot, and people, also, would forget again, as they had done several times before. "Posterity has a right to know how it all happened," he told Ralph. "Write it—or have it written by a professional."

For years, Ralph was hesitant to do just that. We know his reasons; God wasn't ready for it.

There are many, skiers and non-skiers, who are glad that God finally told Ralph Samuelson to overcome his modesty, and get 'agittin' with his records—as he got 'agittin' with his skis.

In short, why did Ralph Samuelson do, or not do, what he did? "Because God planned it that way," said Ralph. "God had other, bigger, more important, more exciting, more world-wide plans for me."

An answer that stops all guessing.

{e}
Epilogue

Normam Holst, one of the most respected public servants of historic Lake City, member of the Lake City Hospital Board for over two decades, president of Kiwanis for many terms, and his vivacious wife, Virginia, were charming hosts at a small intimate gathering in their unique home on South Prairie, not far from the little church where Ralph Samuelson counted the ceiling squares.

The conversation got around to the Father of Water Skiing as it often does in Lake City.

Virginia recalled how she and friends used to run down to the Lake to see "that crazy Sammy" try to slide on water. Virginia's mother, Katherine Mosely, remembered Ralph's mother, Mary—and how hard she worked.

Said Norman, "Ralph's done a lot for Lake City in his time. I wonder if he realizes how much?"

A guest added a comment. "Each of us does his so-called thing as he sees it. Ralph Samuelson did it his way. The interesting point is, he didn't realize what he was doing when he was doing it. He does now. And now he's eager to use all his influence and his prestige to witness for the Lord, convince people that he was, still is, merely a tool. He wants to tell millions of water skiers and their friends, too, that they must become aware of God and His presence. And I don't think anybody can stop him from trying."

Ralph certainly tried. Even as a septuagenarian.

His conversion—or as he liked to think of it, "the Descent of the Holy Ghost into his soul"—took place in the spring of 1947, when he was only 44 years old.

Instead of fading through the years, his convictions became more and more firmly rooted.

He still insisted he knew nothing about theology, reminded his friends that as a boy he got no religious instruction and never read the Bible. God wanted it that way, he believed, so he could write on him later as a clean slate.

"I was one of God's fools," Ralph said often.

When I met him, he selected a lesson entitled, "How to be Foolish," based on I Corinthians 4:9-10, from his favorite monthly *These Days*, published for the Cumberland Presbyterian Church.

"Listen to this," he said. "We have become a spectacle to the world, to angels, and to men. We are fools for Christ's sake."

"That's me. That's me all over. In a way I'm a spectacle to the world. Perhaps not to angels but certainly to men. Twelve million water skiers in the U.S. alone have at least heard my name. But I am still a fool for Christ's sake.

"They called me that, a fool, when I first tried to ski on water. They called me crazy. It hurt, but I let it pass—and never showed my feelings. But it hurt.

"Just as it says here, 'No one likes to be called a fool.' Yet how often some of the world's most useful people are branded by that name: Robert Fulton for his steamboat, Alexander Graham Bell for his talking machine, and Thomas Edison for his incandescent bulb. They were only a few who were considered foolish by their shortsighted contemporaries. How much poorer the world would be without their foolishness.

"Paul and the Apostles also were called fools, but they were fools for Christ's sake. Their foolishness was to live in the example of the Master—bringing love where men had known only hatred, offering help where others did not care, and proclaiming the truth even at the risk of their lives.

"Such foolishness is still needed in the world today. It will always be needed as long as sensible people ignore the way of Christ.

"Now isn't that the only, real wisdom?" Ralph asked.

Samuelson's favorite Biblical character was Paul, formerly Saul. He had always been fascinated by the story of Saul's conversion on the road, to Damascus, when he was blinded by a holy light, went into the desert to ponder about his sins of plotting to kill Christians, came back Paul, one of the greatest witnesses for his Master. Ralph often referred to this story.

When he was made aware that I had been to Damascus, had traveled the very road Saul had been on, had written about the place where Paul was later let down the wall in a basket to escape his enemies in Damascus, Ralph asked eager questions.

Many of Ralph's friends insisted on turning him off, or avoiding him when he got going on his "religious tick."

Ralph didn't mind. He was never obtrusive in his evangelizing, if that's the name for it, any more than he was eager to attract ski glory to himself.

He was not a breast-beating, shouting, gesticulating, pleading sort of Christian, although Ralph was a great admirer of Billy Graham and quoted him often.

He was the quiet type who waited for the proper moment in

a conversation, then calmly remarked that his own life had been a miracle from beginning to end.

Only after questioning, which naturally follows such a challenging word as "miracle," did Ralph Samuelson modestly witness for his Lord, simply by giving him credit for everything: first the skiing itself, the jumping, the speed skiing, the work in Detroit, in Florida, finding Hazel through what he still called divine guidance (something Hazel cherished), the healed back, the money for the education of his children, the hernia that didn't strangle, the rediscovery of his old skis, the rediscovery of Ralph Samuelson, the honors heaped upon him.

It was all a miracle to Ralph Samuelson—God helping him whenever he needed help, giving him health and giving him children.

And this book.

Especially this book, which to Ralph was the greatest miracle of all—his opportunity to witness.

There was one more miracle Ralph prayed for.

The church is not helping people enough. It is not alive enough, spiritually; education is not inspiring our youth enough; government is too big, too self-serving, too lax, too bureaucratic, too short-sighted, too venal; mankind is despairing; morality has gone on the rocks.

All because people have turned away from God, Ralph said.

Man does not listen to Him as He attempts to speak.

Teachers are too permissive, politicians too crooked, business too selfish.

But Life is still a miracle.

And, somehow, Ralph believed that if we prayed for it, God, who has created so many miracles, would create one more and save this nation of ours from itself, convert the materialistic unbelievers who are running it.

Not that Ralph Samuelson thought of himself as perfect.

He admitted it often; he was a sinner.

"We are all sinners before we become real Christians. Then we become new people, have a new life, are changed from within," Ralph proclaimed.

"Yes, indeed. I've had my share of sins, all right. And I'm not proud of them."

He added with candor, "The skeletons in my closet, as some joker once put it, are the kind that are beautiful, shapely, and enticing. Back in Florida I had many affairs with young women; and more, after I came back to Lake City. I am sure many mothers in my hometown were happy when I married my first wife and moved away. I'm not proud of some of those escapades."

"I suppose my problem with girls, which caused me to sin more than anything else, was a temptation which I could have avoided but didn't."

Ralph admitted, in retrospect, to another weakness he had to overcome, his temper—a violent, flaring, red-hot surge of emotions that often expressed itself in curses, and sometimes in physical violence.

"If I were to analyze myself, I would say that my temper was a difficult thing to overcome, even after I became a Christian in the true sense of the word. I still have to fight to keep it under control. I believe someday I will really master it. Of course, I could easily rationalize and say God put me into many situations where he shouldn't have put me and that my curses were natural, but I realize that's no excuse."

"My problem with my temper would have been even worse if I had been a drinker. Thank God, I always shunned liquor. I had always vowed I wouldn't fall into that trap. That's one vow I've kept. But, so help me God, I broke many others—made many mistakes."

The last eight words tell it all.

Ralph himself assuaged his pangs about his past sins by quoting again from *My Utmost for His Highest,* the book I had seen in his home when I first met him.

The lesson refers to I John 3:4, "Whosoever is born of God doth not commit sin. To be born of God means that I have the supernatural power of God to stop sinning," Ralph explained. In the Bible it is never: Should a Christian sin? The Bible puts it emphatically: A Christian must not sin. The effective working of the new birth in us is that we do not commit sin, not merely that we have the power not to sin, but that we have stopped sinning. Does that mean that we cannot sin? "It means that if we obey the life of God in us, we need not sin."

Ralph believed he need not sin. So he didn't, if he could help it.

His favorite Bible quotation was Matthew 21:28-33, the parable of a certain man who had two sons and came to the first and asked him to work in the vineyard. He said, "no" he would not, but later repented and went. The man asked his second son, and he answered, "yes," he'd go. But he didn't.

As Matthew wrote: "Whether of them twain did the will of his father? They say unto Him. The first, Jesus saith unto them. Verily I say unto you, that the publicans and the harlots go into the kingdom of God before you. For John came unto you in the way of righteousness, and ye believed him not; but the publicans and the harlots believed him; and ye, when ye have seen it, repented not afterward, that ye might believe him."

Ralph Samuelson was certain that he believed everything that ever happened to him happened so that he could witness.

He put it succinctly, as usual:

"God gave me the inspiration for my water skiing, and now He wants to use me to reach others through this great experience and the recognition it has brought me. What a wonderful opportunity for me as the Father of Water Skiing to reach millions of people who participate in this wonderful water sport throughout the world.

"Hopefully my words, my warnings, my example, will make people aware that we all have a great power within us, a power that can give us wonderful spiritual love, the "Agape" of the ancient Greeks.

"I know this love can enter our souls. It happened to me. I called on God like Job, and he sent down his Holy Spirit to comfort me. I had lived in sin—but still he accepted me.

"This is a time, as never before, when the world needs a great change—for the better. Truly, religious leaders tell us that unless we as a nation have a spiritual rebirth, a revival of the spirit, soon, we are sure to become a doomed nation. Inflation, dishonesty, crime, use of drugs, the breaking down of the family, the destruction of the sanctity of the marriage vow, vanity, the mad scramble for money, money, money—all are evil things, not worthy of us as a Christian nation.

"God can help you as he helped me; God can give you peace; God can give you strength; God can give you a new life—the desire to live with Him. He can give the whole world this spiritual revival which we so urgently need—if we pray for it."

Ralph had one great worry. He wondered if modern youth would listen. He didn't know what he could do about that.

But one thing he did know. He would always give God all the honor, for everything. He would always remind everybody who would listen, including the millions of young water skiers, as well as the more mature ones, that God's is the Kingdom, the Power, the Glory.

"Before I go, I must witness for the Lord as I now know he wanted me to do, even back in 1922. I didn't hear him. He finally made me listen, after a lot of travail.

"Somebody once called me Job on Water Skis. I am the Father of Water Skiing. I was the first to prove it could be done. But for decades I was completely forgotten, ignored. For more than half of my lifetime, nobody ever heard of me.

"I started poor, without a dime, became rich (not because of my connection with water skiing, however), became conceited, and then went through more tribulations than Job himself. I went bankrupt, losing a $250,000 business and a beautiful farm and home. I broke my back, nearly died several times. I let my family starve.

"And what happened?

"Miracles happened.

"And finally, after decades of anonymity, God permitted me to be rediscovered by what seemed an accident, a sheer coincidence. But it was a miracle.

"Yes, I've lived a whole lifetime of miracles. Inventing water skiing was only one of the first.

"He works in mysterious ways. A lot of people have said that. I've experienced it. It started with two pine boards; it will end with pine boards again—when I'm in my coffin."

Ralph W. Samuelson died in 1977 and was buried in Lake City, as close to his beloved Lake as possible. He chose the words for his grave marker himself: a fitting epitaph to the Lake Pepin pioneer, who always considered his pine board ride into history a real Miracle:

RALPH SAMUELSON
Father of Water Skiing
—
Witness for Christ

{a}
About the Author

GREGOR A. ZIEMER

Gregor Athalwin Ziemer was born May 24, 1899, in Colum-
bia, Mich., into a five-generations-long line of Lutheran min-
isters. His was a more secular calling to education and service,
first as an educator in the Philippines (1926-1928) and then
as founder and headmaster of the American School in Berlin,
Germany, during the pre-World War II years of 1928-1939. He
earned his doctorate at the University of Berlin in 1934.

Ziemer worked as a correspondent for the *Chicago Tribune*,
New York Herald and *London Daily Mail*, writing from his unique
perspective as a spectator living within Adolph Hitler's Nazi em-
pire. After refusing to fly the Swastika in place of the American
flag, Ziemer was forced to leave Germany in 1939.

He returned to America and tucked his family into the hometown of his wife Edna (Wilson) Ziemer—Lake City, Minn.
There, Ziemer wrote his *New York Times* Bestseller book, *Education for Death: The Making of the Nazi* and penned, with young

daughter Patricia, the top selling book *Two Thousand And Ten Days of Hitler*. In 1943, RKO General Productions released *Hitler's Children*, the blockbuster movie based upon Ziemer's work.

In 1945, Ziemer served as a lieutenant colonel in General George Patton's famed 4th Armored Division on its victorious march into Berlin where he broadcasted the news of Hitler's demise and then worked to reestablish a free press in post-war Germany.

After the war, Ziemer became the director of public education at the American Foundation for the Blind where he formed a lasting friendship with Helen Keller. He later served as director of the Institute of Lifetime Learning in Long Beach, Calif., developing curriculum to keep seniors' minds ever active. He also authored a children's book with his wife, *Whirlaway Hopper*, wrote screenplays, contributed to such publications as *Reader's Digest*, *The Saturday Evening Post*, and *Good Housekeeping*, and worked as a lecturer and commentator.

Though they lived in California, the family spent summers in Lake City, Minn., where Ziemer completed his manuscript, *Witness on Water Skis*, in 1975. He did not live to see it published; Ziemer died Aug. 19, 1982, in Rochester, Minn., and is buried in Lake City.

MORE TITLES

available through Hunter-Halverson Press, LLC

Check out some of these titles from

 **THE HERO NEXT DOOR** ®

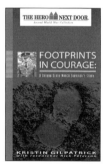

Footprints in Courage
By Kristin Gilpatrick

Read how U.S. Airman Alf Larson survived a tortuous forced hike and nearly 4 years of Japanese brutality and captivity as a prisoner of war during W.W.II.

The Hero Next Door:
The Korean War
By Kristin Gilpatrick

War history author Kristin Gilpatrick moves her biographical story telling of The Hero Next Door® Series to the Korean War and captures the tales of 14 Wisconsin men and women who faced the horrors and homesickness of combat during the 1950-53 United Nations struggle to save South Korea from dreaded communism.

HUNTER
HALVERSON
PRESS-LLC

115 West Main Street, Second Floor • Madison, WI 53703
info@hunterhalversonpress.com